GW00789478

FINDING FRESH LIGHT

Regards, love and
Blessings to you,
Mary

— Joe

Remembering 9/11
and all victims of terror.

Joseph Pollard

Finding Fresh Light

HOMILIES ON THE GOSPELS OF THE SUNDAYS
AND CELEBRATIONS OF CYCLE C

*Above all, it's the gospels that occupy my mind.
I'm always finding fresh lights there.*
— Thérèse of Lisieux, *Autobiography*

the columba press

First published in 2003 by
the columba press
55A Spruce Avenue, Stillorgan Industrial Park,
Blackrock, Co Dublin

Cover by Bill Bolger
Origination by The Columba Press
Printed in Ireland by ColourBooks Ltd, Dublin

ISBN 1 85607 419 6

Acknowledgements
Scripture quotations are taken from The New Revised Standard
Version, copyright (c) 1989, by the Division of Christian Education of
the National Council of the Churches of Christ in the United States of
America. Used by permission.

Copyright © 2003, Joseph Pollard

Contents

Introduction

These are short homilies on the gospels of the Sundays and some celebrations of Cycle C. I concentrate on the core message of the gospel reading and try to apply it to the circumstances in which we live.

The homilies tend to be catechetical. I believe this is a need of the moment. Lack of substantive catechesis is a complaint heard for some time now on both sides of the Atlantic. As a small illustration of this, I watched a TV biography series *as Gaeilge* last year and was surprised at the number of 'our own' who no longer define death and the afterlife in Christian terms.

Christian hope, too, is under stress. Morris West feels that religious people today are silenced by the strength of evil and violence at home and abroad. Evil, he says, is so widespread and so 'serene in its enormity' that it 'makes the face of God invisible.' (*A View From The Ridge*) The homilist, therefore, cannot hide behind inept theological pieties and 'stories going nowhere with the gospel' but tries to address the people's real life environment with Christ's word and Christian hope.

The homilist tries to make the face of God visible. He wishes to be a sign of faith and hope in his own time and place. His homilies try to be small documents of faith and hope. They urge the hearer 'not to be overcome by evil, but to conquer evil with good.' (Rom 12:21) They urge the hearer to continue to put the Lord Jesus forward to our time as the 'invisible face of God made visible'. (cf Col 1:15)

Jesus is the ground of our faith and the assurance of our hope. The homilist is always reinforcing these truths in the hearts of his hearers.

1st Sunday of Advent: Gospel: Lk 21:25-28, 34-36

Always Vigilant

[Jesus said] 'And there will be signs in sun and moon and stars, and upon the earth distress of nations in perplexity at the roaring of the sea and the waves, men fainting with fear and with foreboding of what is coming on the world; for the powers of the heavens will be shaken. And then they will see the Son of Man coming in a cloud with power and great glory ... Be vigilant at all times, praying that you may have strength to escape all these things that will take place, and to stand before the Son of Man.'

When I was small westerns were a feature of Irish town life. Westerns were called cowboy pictures and the local cinema was 'the pictures'. We didn't go to the cinema or the movie palace or the Cineplex: we went to 'the pictures'. The usual fare of the Sunday matinee for children was a trailer (our word for preview) of what was coming next week, a short (often a somewhat aged Pathe or Movietone newsreel), and the feature film. The trailer and the short made up what the home-made poster bills grandly called the 'full supporting programme'.

Our teachers worried about the American slang we were picking up from the likes of Tom Mix and Buck Jones and Hopalong Cassidy. We mimicked the lingo of our heroes. 'Stick 'em up an' han' over the gold!' one of us said with a bent twig for a six-shooter. The stagecoach driver, much too cool and ready to die, said, 'I ain't turnin' no gold over.' Just when the stagecoach driver was about to depart this life, full of lead, the sheriff came from behind a tree and said, 'Drop it, buzzard, or you bite the dust.' Even my father, who read all the Zane Greys that the county library owned, was wary of my Americanisms.

But our parents and teachers, God rest them, were as innocent as ourselves when it came to this supposed adverse American influence. 'Ain't' is not really an Americanism: it was brought to the New World by English immigrants, and biting the dust and licking the dust are biblical expressions. (See Gen 3:14; Ps 72:9)

The same can be said of many of today's expressions. They come down to us from Roman or early Christian times. For example, one finds military units and fire-fighting brigades oper-

8

ating under such biblical mottoes as *Semper Fidelis* (always faithful), *Semper Paratus* (always ready) and *Semper Vigilans* (always vigilant). We find these last words in the final line of today's gospel. As we await his second coming Jesus says, 'Be vigilant always, praying that you may have the strength to escape all these things that will take place, and to stand before the Son of Man.'

Jesus spoke these words of caution when he heard the people's gushing comments about the beauty and the permanence of God's temple in Jerusalem. He warned that God would reject the temple, as it would reject Jesus. He said it would all be thrown down, stone upon stone. Israel itself would be scattered. And all of this would happen in the 'day of the Lord'.

The 'day of the Lord' is a biblical view of the future. The prophet Amos foresaw it as a time of judgement. (5:18-27) Isaiah understood it as the time when God's rule would be established over the earth. (40) There would be a period of upheaval and terror as the present age came to an end and the age of God's universal rule arrived.

Jesus uses these elements in his own view of the 'day of the Lord'. For him too, the 'day of the Lord' is the arrival of God's universal rule in conjunction with his own so-called second coming. For him too, the 'day of the Lord' is prefaced by a period of turmoil and upheaval during which the elements will be convulsed, the nations will be in distress, and men and women will 'die of fright' [NAB wording] as they await what is coming upon them. Other scriptures allow us to include the pain and persecution of Christ's followers in this awful preface period.

The preface period is now. It is already here. We are in it. It is critical for us, then, to endure the trials of this period for they are the cost of Christian discipleship. We can shorten this period and, according to Peter, even 'hasten' the second coming of Christ by our 'holy conduct and devotion'. (2 Pet 3:11-12) All the while we must be vigilant; watching and waiting and ready to receive the Lord when he comes. The Lord asks us for this. In the final book of the Bible he says, 'Behold, I am coming soon. So hold fast to what you have lest someone rob you of your crown.' (Rev 3:11 [NAB])

The Lord's coming may occur at any time. It has been a possibility in every Christian generation, and it may happen in our own. On the other hand we, like the Christian generations which have gone before us, may not meet the Lord in his second coming but in the ordinary process of our own death. Either way, we must be vigilant and ready for Jesus.

Let us, then, not be so rooted in this world as to think it permanent, as others wrongly thought the strong and beautiful Jerusalem temple permanent. The present age is passing away slowly but surely. So, by all means let us build our houses, rear our children, grow our investments and even keep an eye on our pension fund, but not with more energy than we apply to watching and waiting and being ready for the great and glorious coming of the Lord.

Straighten your Lives
as well as your Roads!

The word of God came to John the son of Zechariah in the wilderness; and he went into all the region about the Jordan, preaching a baptism of repentance for the forgiveness of sins. As it is written in the book of the words of Isaiah the prophet, 'Prepare the way of the Lord, make his path straight.'

We are busy at the moment straightening our roads. We are straightening hundreds of roads that were built for the horse. It's an expensive business. And putting in place a national motorway system to achieve an even straighter road is putting ourselves out-of-pocket by the billions of Euro.

John the Baptist, in today's gospel, is also in the business of straightening roads, but in the spiritual and moral sense. He even calls for a motorway of the straightest kind. He is God's engineer. He wants the people to prepare the spiritual road by which the Lamb of God, who is about the make his appearance, may move easily into their hearts. He demands that they build such a highway in place of the crooked roads that the scribes and the Pharisees, and their own compromising lives, have built thus far.

And John wants solid construction. Like a good engineer he wants deep excavation and bedrock foundation. He wants compaction and smooth surfacing. In spiritual terms, he wants real repentance and a renewal of heart. He wants proven virtue and single-minded preparation for the coming of the Lord. He challenges the people to straighten their crooked faith, smooth out their ragged moral lives, level the hills of their pride and fill in the valleys of their omissions. Then the coming Lord may drive effortlessly into their hearts, and they will receive 'the salvation of God'.

All the while John is using imagery and words of the prophet Isaiah (c 40). In Isaiah, the imagery and the words describe the end of the Second Exile (or Babylonian Captivity) of the Jewish people, and their glorious return to Jerusalem. The road of the return is constructed by 'angels'. When it is ready God leads the exiles home. He leads them along the road with the love of the

11

model shepherd, 'carrying the lambs in his bosom and leading the ewes with care.' (40:11) John the Baptist sees himself against this Isaian background. He, too, is an angel (i.e. messenger) of God. He, too, is constructing a road. He is preparing the way of the Messiah. And he is involving the people in its construction. For what is about to come down this road for them is the long-awaited Messiah bringing 'the salvation of God'.

You and I are preparing for the coming of Jesus into our hearts at Christmas. We know full well, regrettably, that Christmas is a cluttered time, even a gridlocked time. We know that this wonderful season has become the frayed and frantic time of the year. It is, then, a real challenge for us to prepare the way of the Lord into our hearts at Christmas. But if we don't, Christmas is robbed of its true meaning and purpose in our regard. So let us take up the challenge of John the Baptist and 'prepare the way of the Lord.' Let us allow our Saviour a straight run into our hearts.

What condition is our spiritual road in? I imagine that, in all our cases, the road could do with a bit of straightening here and a bit of mending there. There is some old hill that still needs a bit of levelling, some dip in need of filling in, some pothole to be patched, some roughness to be made smooth. Perhaps for one or two of us the spiritual road is so damaged that total reconstruction is required through an about-face in our values and lifestyle, and a heartfelt confession of sin. At any rate, as we straighten the roads of our nation, let us not forget the more important straightening of our spiritual and moral lives as well.

Baptised in Fear or with Fire?

As the people were in expectation, and all men questioned in their hearts concerning John, whether perhaps he were the Christ, John answered them all, 'I baptise you with water; but he who is mightier than I is coming, the thong of whose sandals I am not worthy to untie; he will baptise you with the Holy Spirit and with fire.'

Fear can paralyse people. In the early 1930s, when the Depression ruled and people feared for their survival, the Americans elected Franklin D. Roosevelt as their president. He recognised that his nation was in a paralysis of fear. Markets and farms and industries had collapsed. Farmers had invested heavily in machinery and when the banks panicked and called in the loans the crops rotted in the fields.

'In Chicago the garbage was picked over for food by desperate women, competing with flies and maggots.' (Hugh Brogan, *Penguin History of the USA*) In one rural place a family was found eating dandelions. Grandfathers put shotguns to their heads in the dustbowl states and men in pin-striped suits walked out of windows in New York. It is hard for us to imagine America ever being in such a state.

Since the people did not understand what was happening to their bountiful land, and since the good-willed Hoover administration had no recovery plan that worked, fear paralysed the population. The newly-elected Roosevelt recognised this paralysis as his nation's greatest enemy. So in his inaugural address he famously said, 'Let me assert my firm belief that the only thing we have to fear is fear itself.' (4/3/1933)

Coming to our own time, Carlo Carretto writes, 'Fear lives in the city. Fear lives in the church. That the city should be afraid doesn't surprise me: it is natural that it should, given the rising tide of delinquency and the audacity of terrorists and bandits. What worries me is the fear inside the church, for this is a melancholy symptom of the decay of our faith in Christ risen from the dead, in Christ the Lord of history. The post-conciliar church runs the risk of going down in history as the Church of Fear.' (*Summoned by Love*) Carretto goes on to call the church's fear 'a denial of the Holy Spirit'.

Are we the Church of Fear? Does our fear deny the Holy
Spirit? Some form of paralysis does seem to attach itself to us at
the moment. When I proposed something to a bishop some
years ago, he said, 'We have to keep our heads down and ride
out the present storm.' The 'present storm' is the child abuse
tragedy.

What might John mean when he said that Jesus would baptise with the Holy Spirit and with fire? John, we may assume,
was as knowledgeable in Jewish theology as any holy man. He
knew, therefore, certain things about the Holy Spirit. He knew
that the Spirit is God's breath of life. He knew that when the
Spirit breathed into a piece of clay it became a living person. He
knew that this person, given the Spirit of God, has the power to
transform himself and herself from weakness and fearfulness
into a courageous man and woman of God. Was he not himself
living proof of the Spirit's transforming power? He knew that, in
the Spirit, the child of God is able to recognise the truth of God
and the certainty of that truth. And he knew that, in the Spirit,
the child of God is able to recognise personal and collective sins
and excuses for the falsehoods they are.

He knew more. He knew – either from spiritual insight or in-
fused grace – that Christ's form of baptism would add something else to the Spirit's action on the believer. He knew it would
add fire. This fire is the fire which illuminates the believer with
the fullness of God's truth found in Christ. And this fire is the
flame of Christ's love burning in the believer and radiating outward in love of God and neighbour. And this fire is the purifying
fire which forges the new heart and the 'new man' (Eph 4:24), so
that Paul would later say of everyone baptised in the Spirit and
with fire, 'You are a new creation ... you are the temple of the living God.' (2 Cor 6:16) Thus newly constituted by the baptism of
Spirit and fire, the Christian is commissioned to the saving work
of Jesus, to bringing 'all things in the heavens and on earth into
one under Christ's headship.' (Eph 1:7)

Christ's mission is our mission. He has baptised us in his
Holy Spirit and with the Spirit's fire. He invites no one in the
church to confusion, to division, to keeping heads below the
parapet, to the paralysis of fear. He has not invited you and me
and this generation to 'risk going down in history as the Church
of Fear.' Instead, he has baptised us in his Holy Spirit so that we,
like him, might 'cast fire upon the earth.' (Lk 12: 49)

Blessedness

Mary arose and went with haste into the hill country, to a city of Judah, and she entered the house of Zechariah and greeted Elizabeth. And when Elizabeth heard the greeting of Mary, the babe leaped in her womb; and Elizabeth was filled with the Holy Spirit and she exclaimed with a loud cry, 'Blessed are you among women.'

Elizabeth said to Mary, 'Blessed are you among women.' Elizabeth realised that Mary had been chosen above all women to be the mother of the Saviour. We are told that this vocation was the dream of every Jewish girl through all the Jewish generations. Mary alone became its fulfilment.

To be chosen as the mother of the Saviour was to become the fulcrum of history, as Christians understand history. Mary's motherhood is the pivot on which history stops moving in one direction and starts moving in another. For in Jesus, the fruit of Mary's blessedness, 'a new age has dawned, the long reign of sin is ended, a broken world is renewed, and man is once again made whole.' (Easter Preface, IV) Mary is blessed as the woman among all women, as the mother of the Saviour. And we are the happy beneficiaries of her blessedness.

But blessedness is not all sunshine and light. Take Mary's case. Here is the most blessed woman in history and yet how deeply will she not suffer because of it! Imagine, for example, her astonishment when the angel announces, out-of-the-blue, 'You will conceive a son,' and the statement staggers her because she does not know man. Imagine the perplexity of Mary, now clearly pregnant, when her bewildered husband resolves 'to divorce her quietly'. (Mt 1:19) Imagine her journey to Bethlehem, exposed to winter weather and roving bandits, seated on the donkey on a rocky road, and wondering when her water will break. Imagine her giving birth to her child in a cold stall with the soiled straw of the animals for a floor.

Imagine her trauma when Simeon prophesies in the temple that her child will be the downfall of many in Israel, and that he will be a sign of contradiction for his nation. Imagine the shock when he says that a sword will pierce her heart. Imagine the pain when her own relatives say that her son is out of his mind.

Imagine her neighbours saying that he works his miracles through the power of the devil. Imagine her shock at the blood-thirsty mob calling for the release of a murderer and her son's crucifixion.

Imagine her standing helpless at the foot of the criminal's cross in the place where human bones and skulls are left as a sinister warning. Imagine her holding her son's body in her arms as day turns to night and the heavens erupt uncomprehendingly. Imagine her facing the future foresworn by her relatives, her son executed, her husband dead long before her, and the curse of her nation on the day she was born.

Yet these soul-stretching things are part of the condition of Mary's blessedness, part of the life of the one who was 'blessed among women'. Most of us, I'm afraid, have a technicolour view of blessedness, a holy card view of sanctity. We must become more realistic and know that when God chooses a person for blessedness he chooses him or her for a substantial share of his Son's cross. The more blessed one is, I think, the greater the cross one carries to sign it.

You and I, dear people, have comparatively small crosses to carry. Let us commit to carry them well. Let us carry them with faith and in love. Realise that we are now part of a Western culture of comfort which despises crosses and which, in the despising, has come to understand Christ and his mother and genuine Christianity less and less. The state of Christian blessedness is not the crown without a cross nor the cross without a crown. And it never will be. Blessedness is the condition of being chosen by God for the measure of both.

Making Room in the Inn

In those days a decree went out from Caesar Augustus that all the world should be enrolled ... And all went to be enrolled, each to his own city. And Joseph also went up from Galilee, from the city of Nazareth, to Judea, to the city of David, which is called Bethlehem, because he was of the house and lineage of David, to be enrolled with Mary, his betrothed, who was with child. And while they were there, the time came for her to be delivered. And she gave birth to her first-born son and wrapped him in swaddling clothes, and laid him in a manger, because there was no room for them in the inn.

In a more trusting time, when Irish doors stayed invitingly half-open all day, there was a pop song which went something like this: 'The next time you find yourself in our locality/ Try a sample of our hospitality./ There's always room in our house to share a smile or two./ There's always room enough, dear friends, for you.'

In our gospel story we have Joseph and Mary travelling from Galilee in the north down to Bethlehem in Judea to register in the census. The chief purpose of the Roman census was – you might have guessed – taxation. Joseph and Mary travel to Bethlehem because the law requires them to register in the city of Joseph's tribal ancestors.

The journey is no easy one. Bethlehem is eighty miles south of Nazareth. It is winter, and in the semi-desert climate the nights are very cold. The road is just a dirt track. Joseph walks. Mary, traditionally, rides a donkey because her time of deliverance is at hand. Bethlehem is then just a small village on the edge of the Judean wilderness. It is a caravan stop for traders.

When Joseph and Mary get to Bethlehem it is already crowded with travellers and merchants and, no doubt, a handful or more of robbers checking out the caravans and sizing up their future prey. The inn is full and there is no room for them. So they settle down, as best they can, in what was likely the courtyard or the animal enclosure of the inn. In that obscure setting Mary delivers her child, and the Saviour of the world is born.

This story, so simple in its telling and so bare in its surroundings, is a foreshadowing of the child's future. Perhaps it is constructed in this simple and sparse way so that we will not miss the markers that point like ominous fingers to the child's future. The markers are these ... Jesus is not spared, even in his mother's womb. The days and nights preceding his birth are days and nights of uprooting and of the dusty, cold and bandit-ridden road. He is born without midwife or relations to assist him and his mother, in relative abandonment, and in the glare of dumb animals and rough men. He will die as he was born, in relative abandonment, in the gaze of rude and mocking men. His mother 'wraps him in a swaddling cloth and lays him in a manger.' The same gospel writer, Luke, records the end of the child's life with the pointedly parallel line: 'Joseph of Arimathea wrapped the body in a winding cloth and laid it in a tomb.' (Lk 23:53)

Most striking of all is the phrase which tells why the Saviour's birth was so impoverished: 'There was no room for them in the inn.' It sums up the child's future as if it were its prophecy. For despite the fact that, in later years, the people will delight in his miracles and be awe-struck at his teaching and at his transparent goodness, he will never find a home among them. At the end of the day, he will find no room in the inn of their hearts. He will say, 'The foxes have dens, the birds of the air have nests, but the Son of Man has nowhere to lay his head.' (Lk 9:58)

Here we are, you and I, dear friends, on this night of our dear Saviour's birth. He is still looking for a room in the inn. It is still the winter of his discontent and he is still faced with rejection and with the over-crowded hearts of the modern world. Yet he must be born – spiritually – in every generation and in each human heart in order to save it and to cherish it. Have we a room for him? Indeed, we have! Let each of us say on this holy night: 'Maranatha: Come, Lord Jesus!' (Rev 22: 20) Be born in me. There is tonight, and there always will be, a warm room for you in the inn of my loving heart!'

The Mystery of God's Love

The Word became flesh and dwelt among us, full of grace and truth; and we have beheld his glory, glory as of an only Son from the Father ... And from his fullness we have all received, grace upon grace. For the Law was given through Moses; grace and truth came through Jesus Christ. No one has ever seen God: the only Son, who is in the bosom of the Father, he has made him known.

I wish you, dear people, a blessed Christmas. May it mean the birth of Jesus in the stable of your heart with all his healing and comfort and love for you and for those you hold dear.

Some of us here this morning are not regular churchgoers anymore; some of us still are. Even among the regulars there are, most likely, many shades of faith. That may be because our faith has been bruised a bit by a failed marriage, or by our children's fall from faith despite our prayers, or by the church's recent performance, or by the scandal of religious hate and terrorism, or by the growing secularisation of society which whittles away at our spiritual core. Those of us who are not regular churchgoers may be so for no greater reason than that we've lost the habit of it somewhere along the road of life. In all of our cases, the heart has its reasons for whatever deep or shallow faith we swim in, and I am no one's judge. Rather, I'd like to be your support in some small way.

All of us came here to church this morning despite our varying degrees of faith. This means that Christmas is still important to us, whatever our motives for being here. We may wonder if we're really here just to please the spouse, or the kids, or to keep tongues from wagging, or because of custom, sentiment, nostalgia and the ghost of a dearly loved granny. Perhaps it doesn't matter all that much. Perhaps any one of these less than perfect motives is, nonetheless, the grace that God uses to draw us here in worship so that he may touch us once more with his love.

You may wonder if Christmas is just the Christian makeover of an old pagan feast. (The early church made a habit of doing things like that!) You may wonder if Christmas is just the echo of an earlier human form of winter celebration. You may wonder if Christmas is largely based on the gathering long ago of the family, the tribe, round a roaring fire to affirm life at the lowest time of the year and to shake a collective fist in the face of the frosty god of winter. John, in today's gospel, says that Christmas is much more. He says it's the celebration of the mystery of God's love for you and for me. Christmas means that God's love took human form in the baby born in the stable in Bethlehem. In this way, God made his invisible love for us visible, his intangible heart tangible.

In today's gospel, John speaks of Christmas with the hindsight of the years he spent in the company of the Christmas child which grew up and became Jesus of Nazareth. It is John's experience of Jesus of Nazareth that allows him to tell us that the Christmas baby is more than a helpless babe in the straw. The baby is the beginning human form of Word of God full of grace and truth. The life and the ministry of the adult Jesus proved it for John. Jesus turned out to be the forgiveness of God for us poor sinners and God's warmth and love and light in the darkness of our winter world.

Jesus turned out to be the power by which John – and you and I – are able to answer the age-old questions that trouble our friends and contemporaries and maybe even ourselves at times: 'What's it all about? Why am I here? What might give deeper meaning and purpose to my life? Who can guarantee me a future beyond the grave that seems to end everything?'

John found his answers in the baby of Bethlehem who became Jesus of Nazareth. We and our questioning friends can too. In Jesus we are able to live lives of purpose and fulfilment and inner joy. Jesus is the pattern and the power of what each one of us is called to be and can be: a graced human being, a child of God, a person with purpose, someone with a future.

We are worthwhile. Christmas means that we are very worthwhile in God's eyes.

For all our bruises and our failures and our sins, and whether we are regulars or irregulars in our faith and at Sunday worship, we are called by God and we are the beloved of God. You and I, dear friends, are worth the Christmas that God's love makes possible for us. That is what the infant in the crib is telling each one of us this happy Christmas morning.

House and Home

After three days they found [Jesus] in the temple, sitting among the teachers, listening to them and asking them questions ... And his mother said to him, 'Son, why have you treated us so? Behold, your father and I have been looking for you anxiously.' And he said to them, 'How is it that you sought me? Did you not know that I must be in my Father's house?' And they did not understand the saying which he spoke to them. And he went down with them and came to Nazareth, and was obedient to them.

In these days of the decent economy you see the sign 'House for Sale' all over the place. Perhaps you're as struck as I am by the real estate agent's sales superlatives. Every house is guaranteed 'luxurious living' and even the claustrophobic city flat is somehow a 'luxury apartment'.

Now and then I see the touch of our Americanisation. There is a growing shift from 'flat' to 'apartment'. And sometimes I see a 'Home for Sale' among all the 'Houses for Sale'. In America one never sells a house, one only sells a home. It is not an exact designation but it is more engaging from the point of view of sales psychology. I would hazard a guess that some day soon there will be no more flats or houses for sale in Ireland!

Home is somewhere special. Home is where the heart is. Be it ever so humble, there's no place like it. 'Home is where, if you have to go there, they have to let you in.' Home is 'something you somehow haven't to deserve,' writes Robert Frost in *The Death of the Hired Man*. These are wonderful descriptions of what a home represents. And yet they hardly do it justice. For home goes to the depth of who we are and of where we come from. Home is our roothold. Its memories are our inspiration and the life force of our continuing history.

In material terms Joseph and Mary gave Jesus the best home they could afford. In spiritual terms they gave him a memorable home through their love and its effect on his growth and development. They also did everything for him that God's law required of them as parents. And that is why, today, they take him with them to Jerusalem for the feast of Passover. For he has

reached his twelfth year, and he is now eligible to take his place
with the men in the temple.

They are a day's journey on the road home from Jerusalem
when they discover that he is missing. You and I might wonder
why it took them so long to discover this. The reason is simple.
When a family, and the extended family, travelled on treks to
Jerusalem it was just one small part of a large caravan or convoy.
When Mary and Joseph can't find Jesus among their own relatives or in the convoy, they go back to Jerusalem in search of
him. They find him in the temple 'sitting among the teachers ...
asking them questions'. He is not lecturing the doctors of the
law and showing them up with his divine brilliance, as we
might piously think, but learning from them. They are the ex-
perts in God's law, and the boy Jesus wants to know all about it.
Yet they are amazed at the calibre of the questions asked by this
boy of twelve.

Mary says, 'Your father and I have been looking for you anxiously.' He answers, 'Did you not realise that I must be in my
Father's house?' These words need not be taken as a slight to his
mother or a put-down of Joseph, his foster-father; instead, they
reflect Jesus' realisation that God is his Father, and uniquely so.
One gets the feeling that Jesus also discovered, while in his
Father's house, a new depth of delight in God's law. He wanted
the temple doctors to tell him everything about it because he delighted in it, and because he had intimations that he was born
into this world 'not to destroy the law but to fulfil it'. (Mt 5:17)
He discovered, in his Father's house, his vocation as one of service to, and ministry with, the word of God.

You and I are formed by the home we come from and by this
house of God, our parish church, which we attend weekly or
even daily. We wish the same fashioning of home and house of
God for our children. So, today, we challenge ourselves to keep
on providing the best home we possibly can for our children and
cherishing them with our love. We accept that there will be anxious moments, as Mary and Joseph discovered in regard to their
own child.

And we challenge ourselves to see this parish church as our
Father's house, the place where he is present with us, the place
where we and our children feel at home, the place where the
liturgy and the sacraments soothe and strengthen us, where
God's word is proclaimed and explained in a way that delights

us, and the place where all the significant steps and stages of our lives are noted with love and celebrated with grace.

May our children find their roothold in our homes and in this house of God. And may the graced memories of both places be their lasting memories and the life force of their continuing histories.

A New Year Resolution

[The shepherds] found Mary and Joseph, and the babe lying in a manger. And when they saw it they made known the saying which had been told them concerning this child; and all who heard it wondered at what the shepherds told them. But Mary kept all these things, pondering them in her heart.

May I wish you a happy and a blessed New Year. It's that time again when we make New Year resolutions, and hope they last till next week anyway!

The usual resolutions are again staking their claims at the court of our conscience. There's that midriff bulge that calls for a diet. There's that shortness of breath calling for regular exercise. There's that short fuse that gave everybody in the family their Christmas-on-the-edge. There's that near-accident on Stephen's Day that just might be attributable to drink even though you remember having only one or two. And there's still the same old crowd at the office waiting to suffer through another year from your shadow side.

What to do? What to do? The gospel tells us that, about this time of year, Mary was also pondering things in her heart. She was pondering the things she heard the shepherds say about her child. Another translation reads that she was 'treasuring' these things in her heart. What things was she treasuring? Just one sentence, really. The angels told the shepherds, 'For you is born this day ... a Saviour, who is Christ the Lord.' (v 11) This line is the original Christian gospel, the 'good news' from God. (v 10) Jesus is our Saviour and Jesus is the Lord. It is these staggering definitions of her child – Saviour and Lord – that Mary ponders and that Mary treasures about this time of year.

Later on, the church will keep these staggering definitions that Mary pondered and treasured as the centrepiece of its creed, or profession of faith. For it is Jesus, and him only, that 'God has put forward in expiation by his blood' for our sins. (Rom 3:25) He alone is the world's Saviour, and 'there is no other name under heaven ... by which we must be saved.' (Acts 4:12) It is because of his saving service in our regard that God exalts Jesus as the Lord in glory. 'Let the whole house of Israel know with assurance that God has made Jesus both Christ and Lord.' (Acts 2:36) Jesus is our Saviour and Jesus is the Lord. This original and fundamental Christian gospel has gone missing in much of the Western world. It has little real meaning even in many Christian lives today.

Why has it gone missing and why has it little meaning for some of us? There are many possible reasons. And there may be no malice in any of them. Maybe it has gone missing because we feel we have no worthwhile sins and therefore we feel no great need of a Saviour. We define real sin by using the backdrop of TV's daily doses of bombs and bullets and inquiries and tribunals. Against this backdrop, we find little real sin coursing through our veins or troubling the small private world we inhabit. Or maybe it's because the claims of so many religions and deities these days, and the ecumenical respect we must show them, lessen our sense of the uniqueness of Jesus as the sole Saviour and Lord.

Or perhaps our present-day personal and economic concerns in health, careers, business, housing, transportation, etc., push the traditional religious agenda to the side and we feel the need of a set of social saviours different from the traditional religious One we have relied upon. There are many reasons why the original Christian gospel of Jesus as sole Saviour and Lord has gone missing in some lives.

One New Year resolution that we might consider is this image in today's gospel of Mary pondering and treasuring what the angels said to the shepherds about her son. He is the long-awaited Saviour. And he is the Lord. He is your personal Saviour and your loving Lord. By God's decree, all of human history and all our personal histories must pass through him. Otherwise they pass into nothingness.

Resolve, then, to spend a little time each day reading the gospel at home, quietly pondering its relevance to your personal, economic and social life, and treasuring in your heart the words of salvation and of love that Jesus speaks to you through its pages. All of us, these hectic days, need a deeper encounter with the Lord of our lives and of our personal histories. The Little Flower wrote in her autobiography, 'Above all, it's the gospels that occupy my mind. I'm always finding fresh lights there.' You will too, concerning yourself and your life, and your relationship with your sole Saviour and Lord.

The Big Issue

The Word became flesh and dwelt among us, full of grace and truth; and we have beheld his glory, glory as of the only Son from the Father.

I was visiting a man in another parish in the months before he died. The family had contacted me because the man knew me when we were children. He had lost the faith a long time ago. They hoped I could 'bring him round' as the end drew near.

I didn't think I could, but I kept that to myself. He had lived too long away from faith and too much inside his own argument-ative head. He had never developed a companionship with Christ. In truth, he did not know Jesus in any worthwhile way. We talked mostly about childhood. I ended each visit, 'Is there anything that you'd like me to do for you?' There never was other than that I would come again.

In the end, there was no death-bed conversion. He just asked me to 'take care of things' when the time came. He would be buried from his parish church and laid to rest among his own people as was customary. His words were not a statement of personal faith but of accommodation to family, friends and cult-ure. He is one of many such souls in our parishes these days.

During our last visit he said, 'I stopped believing in a God who is useless.' He meant, I think, that he could not accept a God who had no interest in doing anything about this awful world and its suffering, famines, wars, brutality, hate and general human madness. This was the big issue for him, the issue of a supposedly disinterested and disconnected God. It is an issue as old as the philosophers and one which troubles ordinary people in their private thoughts. Naturally, I respect anyone's right to hold this view of a disinterested God if they so wish. But I do not share it despite all the data which one may gather in support of it, for one can bring at least equal data to bear against it.

St Paul strikes me as someone who was aware of the big issue, someone well aware of the dark side of life. He was a real-ist for all his mystical experiences, and he had some very dark stuff in his own earlier history. He had such things as his bigoted attacks on Christians and his role in the murder of Stephen. We find this 'first edition' Paul in every generation. We find him in the bullies and the bigots and the thugs and the tormentors and the abusers and the exterminators.

And then there was the evil done to Paul after he became a Christian: the in-house jealousy, the suspicions, the whisperings; and the lashings, the imprisonments, the hunger and the shipwrecks. For all of that darkness, he insisted that God is dynamically interested and involved in our world and in ourselves especially through Christ. Paul knew the transforming power of grace in his own life and the possibility of its transforming power in ours. Therefore, he could say with utmost realism, 'Do not be overcome by evil but conquer evil with good.' (Rom 12:21) He also said, 'Jesus is the image of the invisible God' (Col 1:15) If Jesus is the image of the invisible God then God is not useless or detached from the world. God entered our world in the person of Jesus in order to save it. In Jesus, Paul said, 'we have strength for everything.' (Phil 4:13)

Paul knew perfectly well that the world is out-of-kilter and that suffering, war, brutality, murder, corruption and madness distort it. The pre-Christian Saul did some of these things himself and the Christian Paul suffered from them. Yet he believed that everything was 'restorable in Christ'. (Eph 1:10) For Christ is the power and the grace to build the better world, and we are his energy and his hands in the work of rebuilding and restoration.

Nothing is achieved for the betterment of the world by sitting in our soft chairs or living in our argumentative heads and dismissing God as disinterested and useless, or by listing the evils of the world as if this naming of shame were the cure of it. Nothing is achieved by removing ourselves from the struggle and retiring into silence and submission, standing on the sidelines full of politeness and impotency, and merely proving the observation of Morris West that evil succeeds because 'good folk are much less certain of themselves than evil ones.' (*A View From The Ridge*) The invisible God made himself visible in the person of Christ and proved himself to be a dynamic and a transforming God. We are called to believe in and to imitate such a God, for he alone is the true God.

Each generation needs to be told that evil is not glorious, that evil people and evil schemes are not good people and good schemes, and that darkness is not light. Each generation needs to be told that God may be by his nature invisible, but that he has made himself visible and involved with us and our problems through Christ. As today's gospel states, he 'became flesh and dwelt among us, full of grace and truth.' The big issue really is that too many today do not look for God where he is to be found, in the face and the heart and the direction and the healing hands of Christ.

The Gifts of the Magi

Then Herod summoned the wise men secretly and ascertained from them what time the star appeared; and he sent them to Bethlehem, saying, 'Go and search diligently for the child, and when you have found him bring me word, that I too may come and worship him.' When they had heard the king they went their way; and lo, the star which they had seen in the East went before them, till it came to rest over the place where the child was. When they saw the star, they rejoiced exceedingly with great joy; and going into the house they saw the child with Mary his mother, and they fell down and worshipped him. Then, opening their treasures, they offered him gifts, gold and frankincense and myrrh. And being warned in a dream not to return to Herod, they departed to their own country by another way.

Epiphany means the showing forth. In this lovely story of the magi (or wise men or kings or astrologers) Jesus is presented as the Saviour of all the nations and not just of his own people Israel. In Jesus there is equal opportunity of grace and salvation for everyone, of all colours and cultures and times, because everyone is equal and deserving in the eyes of the loving God who made all of us his children.

The scripture itself does not tell us the number of the wise men but tradition sets it at three. This number corresponds with the number of the gifts offered to the infant Jesus. The wise men may have been astrologers (as well as kings and wise men) because, as Daniel Harrington notes in his commentary, they possessed astronomical and astrological knowledge. They were stargazers. The unusual star which they observed in the East and then followed 'may have been the conjunction of the planets Jupiter and Saturn'. Whatever it was, they found it novel and startling and its brightness was compelling enough to set them off on their great voyage of spiritual discovery.

King Herod, of course, lies to magi. He does not want them to find the child and report back to him so that he may go and worship the infant, but that he may go and murder the infant. For Herod has heard the rumours that Jesus is born 'king of the Jews' and he is 'troubled' by the news and determined to eliminate a rival to his throne and to his family.

The gifts which the magi offer the child are gold, frankincense and myrrh. Early Christian tradition interpreted each gift as matching 'some characteristic of Jesus and his work.' (William Barclay) Gold symbolises Jesus' kingship. Incense symbolises his divinity. In Barclay's view the incense also symbolises his priestliness because frankincense was used in the temple worship of the priests. Myrrh is prophetic of the child's future death since myrrh is a resin that was used in perfume and in the anointing of the body for burial.

Like the magi, we too are stargazers. Ours is the star-struck generation. We follow stars all over the place and cannot seem to live without them. In fact, stars lead us by our noses. We follow movie stars, pop stars, sports stars, soap stars, and even the stars up there in the sky. But, as St Paul wisely notes, stars are not equal and 'one star differs from another star in glory'. (1 Cor 15:41) The magi challenge us to follow their star, the star of Bethlehem, the brightest star in their firmament and surely in ours too. For the brightest star is Christ the Lord. He is our sole Saviour and our only lasting and saving star in the long run.

And the gifts the magi offered challenge us to give Jesus our most prized gold, which is the love of our heart; the incense which is worship of God and genuine prayer from the heart; and the myrrh which is our continuing works of sacrifice and of love in regard to others, especially in regard to the least of God's children.

Commissioned to Serve

Now when all the people were baptised, and when Jesus also had been baptised and was praying, the heaven was opened, and the Holy Spirit descended upon him in bodily form, as a dove, and a voice came from heaven, 'You are my beloved Son; with you I am well pleased.'

This gospel passage tells us that John the Baptist baptised Jesus. How can that be? Jesus was the sinless one. He had no sin. He had nothing to repent of and to be washed of. Thus John was surprised when Jesus presented himself for baptism. Matthew's gospel says that John even tried to prevent Jesus from undergoing baptism. (cf 3:14)

How are we to understand his baptism then if he didn't need it? One possible understanding is that Jesus underwent baptism as an act of solidarity with his fellow-Jews who were flocking to John. John had stirred them to repentance and Jesus wished to encourage them in what they were doing.

A second possible understanding is that Jesus was capitalising on the new religious fervour, that he was taking advantage of this groundswell of fervour in order to shape it to his own mission as the Messiah. Barclay puts it more graciously by quoting Shakespeare, 'There is a tide in the affairs of men, which, taken at the flood, leads on to fortune.' (*Julius Caesar*, IV, iii)

A third possible understanding, and a more engaging and more likely one, may be found by looking at the first reading of the Mass today. It gives us the opening lines of Isaiah, chapter 42. These lines make up the first of the so-called songs of the Messianic Servant. Jesus is the Servant of God and the 'Man for others' in Dietrich Bonhoeffer's well-known phrase. His baptism is likely a ritual cleansing to mark the start of his Servant ministry. And it is his public statement of the ministry he is about to embark upon with full acceptance and lasting commitment. The Lord's baptism is a statement about service to others. He is commissioned to serve. So are we as a consequence of our own baptism. When Jesus emerges from the water the Spirit descends upon him to seal his commitment, and the voice of the Father announces, 'You are my beloved Son; with you I am well pleased.'

One of the early scholars involved in modern Jesus studies
was the Nobel Prize winner Albert Schweitzer. He was a man of
wide ability in theology, medicine and music. He remains, for
example, even today, the definitive interpreter of Bach's music.
At the pinnacle of European scholarship he dropped everything,
went to Africa, and built a leper hospital on the bank of a river.
There he put into practice his revolutionary Christian insight:
reverence for life on all levels and in all its forms. Schweitzer
hoped that we would discover the secret of a happy life. He said
it is service to others. He hoped we would make the discovery
early in our lives lest we make it only at the door of death, with
wistful regret. Jesus is the Servant of God and the Servant of
others' needs. We are too, in solidarity with him.

The main elements of Christian service are found in the
Servant songs of Isaiah, in the commandments and beatitudes of
Jesus, and in the examples given us through Jesus' ministry. The
old catechism restated these as 'the spiritual and corporal works
of mercy'. We are strong on the corporal works today such as
feeding the hungry, clothing the naked, and visiting our less fortunate brothers and sisters who are ill or in prison. Even the so-
called secular world is greatly involved in these corporal works.

But we may not be all that strong on the spiritual works, especially knowledge of the faith. Many people seem to know little
of substance about the faith. Therefore, you and I should challenge ourselves with regard to the spiritual works. Are we in-
structing the present-day widespread ignorance of the faith?
Are we counselling and encouraging and challenging, as needs
be, those among family members and friends and parishioners
who have doubts of faith and experiences of abuse, addiction,
and moral difficulty of various kinds? Are we pulling our
weight for Christ and his kingdom values in the modern mar-
ketplace of ideas and lifestyles where others, with so much less
to offer, are confidently active? It's our call.

There is no reason why we should fail to see our baptism in
Christ, like his in the Jordan, as our statement of service to others
for the sake of the kingdom of God.

A Time of Testing

And Jesus, full of the Holy Spirit, returned from the Jordan, and was led by the Spirit for forty days in the wilderness, tempted by the devil ... And the devil took him up, and showed him all the kingdoms of the world in a moment of time, and said to him, 'To you I will give all this authority and their glory ... if you will worship me, it shall all be yours.' Jesus answered him, 'It is written, "You shall worship the Lord your God, and him only shall you serve".'

Today we'll look at the second of the three temptations that Our Lord underwent. The devil showed him all the kingdoms of the world in a moment of time and said to him, 'I will give you all of this if you bow down and worship me.'

This temptation is not so much the temptation of power as the temptation to compromise. The devil invites Jesus to compromise the very first commandment of God's law, the commandment that God alone is God and he alone is to be worshipped and adored.

The devil pretends to possess the authority and the power of God. He shows Jesus all the kingdoms of the world in a moment of time as if he were their owner and had the right to dispose of them as he wished. He offers Jesus all of these kingdoms. It is an offer of immense power and wealth. But Jesus must pay a price for it. He must compromise the truth. And he must compromise himself as the Son of God and put Satan in his Father's place and worship him. The devil has, indeed, great power in his own right but he does not have this much power. He is not God and Jesus knows it. Jesus sees through him. The devil is, in fact, not the great Lord God but the Great Pretender.

History is full of pretenders, mere mortals wanting to be gods or pretending to be gods, men of massive egos and matching ambitions. We think of such people as Stalin and Hitler. They acted as though they were gods. They pretended prodigious insights and talents and destinies. They wielded immense power. But their fruits were war and death and destruction on the grand scale. Lord Acton would not have been surprised at their destructive works. He is the source of the famous observation that 'power tends to corrupt, and absolute power corrupts absolutely.' And he added, 'Great men are almost always bad men.' (*Historical Essays & Studies*) Even a little power tends to corrupt. Even a little power can turn our heads in the direction of compromise and pretence and sham and cover-up – and heartbreak for others. We are well aware of the damage these four little gods have done recently in state and church and banking and business life.

Jesus rejects the offer of power and its price tag of compromise. He is God's Son and he will remain true to his Father and faithful to his own mission. These words, faithful and true, are of the very character of Our Lord. We come upon them in the final book of the Bible when the visionary John sees the heavens opened, and as he looks he sees 'a white horse' and on it 'its rider called 'Faithful and True'. And the name of the rider is 'the Word of God'. (Rev 19: 11-13)

You and I know that much of the living of our lives necessarily involves a measure of compromise. Political life, social life and family life are not possible without compromises. Such compromises are acceptable when they are a matter of finding mutually agreeable solutions to difficulties and when they do not involve moral principles as such. The kind of compromise that Our Lord refuses is the compromise of God's truth and moral principle.

We have just begun our Lent, reflecting the forty days of fasting and testing which Jesus underwent in the wilderness. It is a good time to examine our hearts and to review the issue of compromise in our lives. It is a good time to name for ourselves those Christian teachings and principles which must remain beyond compromise and pretence in our personal lives and in our society.

A Preview of Our Future

Jesus took with him Peter and John and James, and went up on the mountain to pray. And as he was praying, the appearance of his countenance was altered, and his raiment became dazzling white.

The incident in today's gospel is the transfiguration of Jesus on the mountain. The transfiguration means that the ordinary form of Jesus – how the disciples saw him day by day – was replaced for a short time by another and quite extraordinary form. It means that the apostles saw Jesus in a way they had not seen him before. They saw a side of him that was hidden until now. They saw the glory that is his as the eternal Son of God.

Jesus is about to go to Jerusalem and to his death. He goes up the mountain to pray to his Father before this most critical event in his life. He wants to know if his approaching sacrificial death is truly necessary. Must he undergo it? Is it really the Father's will? When the transfiguration is over the Lord knows that Calvary is necessary, and he is steeled in heart and spirit to sacrifice his life for us.

His apostles also need to know something. They need some deeper insight into who their Jesus is. They need to know that he is much more than the persuasive rabbi and the great miracle worker they are familiar with. And they need reassurance that the scandal they will soon find in the cross is not the end; that it is necessary; and that all will end in glory for their Lord and for themselves. He and they are part of God's dearest project – the salvation of the world – and glory will follow the scandal of the cross.

And so, the Lord is transfigured in glory before their eyes. His face shines like the sun and his clothes become radiantly bright. Moses' face once shone in similar fashion on Mt Sinai reflecting the glory of God. (Ex 34:29) No doubt, the apostles connected the two events immediately, but they would also have noticed the difference. Only the face of Moses reflected the glory of God on Sinai whereas Our Lord's entire person is bathed in glory on the mount of transfiguration. The apostles see a new Jesus on the mountain. It is a preview, as it were, of his future glory beyond the cross.

Moses and Elijah are present. They represent the Law and the Prophets. They are in conversation with Jesus. What are they saying? Perhaps they are reviewing the scriptures with him and the age-old hope of salvation that will be realised only in the Lamb of God. Perhaps they are offering him reassurances as to his cross, and through it his crown.

Peter is so mesmerised by the whole scene that he wants to set-up three booths or tents. He recalled, no doubt, that the Israelites lived in tents in the wilderness on the way to the Promised Land, and that they would live in tents again – so it was believed – in the Messianic age.

A bright cloud overshadows them. It is the *shechinah*, the luminous cloud that went before the Israelites during the exodus, the cloud that signalled the presence with them of the glory of the Lord. A voice speaks out of the cloud confirming Jesus as God's beloved Son. Our Lord is strengthened and confirmed as to his unique Sonship, his necessary cross, and his glorious future beyond it, and because of it. The lesson for us can hardly be different. Carrying our daily cross with faith, in imitation of Jesus, is our own prelude to glory.

Transfiguration means that there is another level to our Christian lives, a dimension that is yet to be. And what a glorious one it is! What happened to Jesus on the mountain will happen to you and to me. One day, being faithful, we shall be transformed in everlasting glory. We shall be, to use the words of W. B. Yeats, 'changed, changed utterly'. (*Easter 1916*)

The Last Chance Gospel

Jesus told this parable: 'A man had a fig tree planted in his vine-yard; and he came seeking fruit on it and found none. And he said to the vinedresser, "Lo, these three years I have come seeking fruit on this fig tree, and I find none. Cut it down; why should it use up the ground?" And he answered him, "Let it alone, sir, this year also, till I dig about it and put on manure. And if it bears fruit next year, well and good; but if not, you can cut it down".'

If you drive through the southwestern states of America you discover that you are driving through basically desert land. The dark green that sidewalled your car as you cut through the Rockies on the way west gives way to bleached greens and tans and parched yellows over the course of the miles. When you reach the borax-streaked grey of the depressions, you are in the desert proper. The landscape is flat and monotonous. Townships become fewer and farther between. The road is a straight line losing itself on the horizon where the sky and the earth are in-separable in the shimmering heat. You cannot measure distance. Finally, even single houses peter out.

It isn't long until you meet an eye-catching sign which says Next Gas/Water – 60 Miles. It gets ominous when the sign reads Last Chance Gas/Water – 100 Miles. It is said that there are no atheists in foxholes. There can't be too many either on a pencil-like desert road, in the middle of nowhere, with the temperature gauge going up and the petrol gauge going down, and under a baking sun that is doing its best to teach you and your car a les-son in the fragility of life. When you see that Last Chance sign you had better pay attention!

Some people call today's gospel the gospel of the last chance. The owner comes up to the vinedresser and complains about a fig tree that hasn't produced anything in three years. 'Cut it down,' he says. 'All it's doing is taking up good space.' But the vinedresser says, 'Give it another year. Give it one last chance. I'll tend it myself. Then if it fails to produce fruit, it can be cut down.'

What lesson may we take from this parable? Parables, as you know, are stories taken from everyday life. They have an obvious or surface meaning but they also have a more important spiritual meaning. And the spiritual meaning is the intended meaning. The obvious or surface meaning of this parable is that you can only do one of two things with a fruit tree which is consistently fruitless. You can either get rid of it or you can give it another chance. The tree in the story is given another chance. It is given its last chance. If it fails again it will be cut down.

The spiritual meaning of the parable involves a person or a group being given another chance to be spiritually productive. It will be their last chance. What spiritually unproductive person or group is being offered one more chance? Very likely it's the Jewish people and their leaders because the Lord's accusatory parables are most often directed at them. In the spiritual meaning of the parable, God is the owner of the vineyard and Jesus is the vinedresser. Jesus is the one who suggests that the barren tree be given another chance. He elects to fertilise it, to give it special treatment, to tend it with his concern and his love, with his word and his grace, so it may finally become productive.

That was then. What about now? The tree may be understood as any one of us, or any group among us, who is spiritually unproductive. Church and kingdom may be taken as the present-day version of God's vineyard. The barren fig tree is any of us in church and kingdom who is fruitless with the word of God and his grace. We have been given much in being given God's word and his enabling grace. Yet we produce nothing, or less than we should, by way of grateful return. The parable is challenging us to receive the word of God and grace in such a responsive way that they become the root and nourishment of a vibrant spiritual life and of much goodness.

A Christian rooted in the word of God and corresponding with the grace of God should produce much fruit. Yet we fail to be as productive as we might for any number of reasons and mostly, perhaps, because of laziness and the lack of a generous heart. We can do so much better with the talents and the graces God gives us. But let us end on an encouraging note. Today's gospel may be the gospel of the last chance but it is, equally I think, a gospel of great encouragement and of hope. Jesus makes himself the tender of the tree that is you and me, and he stakes his reputation with the Father on the fruit that he is confident he can produce from us.

The Forgiving Father

Jesus said, 'There was a man who had two sons; and the younger of them said to his father, "Father, give me the share of property that falls to me." And he divided his living between them. Not many days later, the younger son gathered all he had and took his journey into a far country, and there he squandered his property in loose living. And when he had spent everything, a great famine arose in that country, and he began to be in want ... and no one gave him anything. But when he came to himself he said, "I will arise and go to my father ..." While he was yet at a distance, his father saw him and had compassion, and ran and embraced him and kissed him ... and said to his servants, "Bring quickly the best robe, and put it on him; and put a ring on his hand, and shoes on his feet; and bring the fatted calf and kill it, and let us eat and make merry; for this my son was dead, and is alive again; he was lost, and is found".'

We have a hard time with forgiveness. We forgive, or think we have forgiven, only to find out years later that we only half-forgave. Even the priest, Mr Collins, in Jane Austin's *Pride And Prejudice* counsels a form of half -baked forgiveness in the name of Christ. 'You ought certainly to forgive them, as a Christian, but never to admit them in your sight or allow their names to be mentioned in your hearing.'

Today's gospel tells the story of a young man who doesn't deserve his father's forgiveness. He couldn't care less about his father. All he wants is a good time and the loot to finance it. He wants his share of his inheritance before he's done any work that might make him even half-worthy of it. He's sick of home and the farm. He's in love with the bright lights of the big city in another country. So off he goes and blows his share of the inheritance in a couple of wild, wanton years.

Then famine strikes that country. Food is in short supply. His erstwhile friends disappear, and his employer will not allow him even the scraps that he feeds to the pigs. Finally, the young man comes to his senses. Here I am, he says to himself, perishing of hunger while my father's servants back home have plenty. So he decides to go home. He does not expect his father to take him back as a son, nor even as one of his regular servants, but he

hopes he will take him back as a hired hand or day labourer. His
father spots him coming 'a long way off'. 'A long way off' suggests that the father had pined for his son from the day he left
and that he went to some piece of high ground every day and
scanned the horizon in hope of his son's return. Before the son
even gets near the house or has the chance to ask forgiveness, his
father is moved to his depths, runs out to meet him, and flings
his arms around his neck and kisses him. Then he orders the servants to bring out the best robe and put it on his boy, and a ring
for his hand, and shoes for his feet. Barclay tells us the symbolism of these items. The robe stands for honour, the ring for authority, and shoes for sonship rather than servanthood. The fatted calf stands for the son's return to be classed as an event
which must be celebrated with great joy.

But what is the spiritual meaning of the story, for this is the
meaning that matters? We – you and I – are the prodigal son.
God is the loving and forgiving Father. Even before we turn our
faces from our sins, his face is already turned in love and forgiveness to us. And his forgiveness is not measured. It is not the
half-forgiveness of Mr Collins. It is full forgiveness. Our being
fully forgiven returns us to our place of grace and destiny in the
kingdom of God. And God is overjoyed to the point of tears at
our return because we are his children and we remain the priority of his heart. How amazingly loved and precious is each one
of us in the eyes of God! That is what Jesus is telling us through
this beautiful story. And it is, by the way, not only a beautiful
Christian story but one of the great short stories in world literature.

We might do two things by way of grateful response. First,
we might spend a little time today letting our preciousness in
God's eyes sink in. We don't appreciate that fact enough. No one
treasures us quite like God our Father. And second, we might
ask our forgiving Father to help us to forgive fully those who
have hurt us seriously with a hurt that still lingers. For if the hurt
still lingers it may be the sign that our forgiveness is imperfect,
and we do not wish to live by Mr Collins' caution that we should
forgive but not abide the sight of the one who hurt us, nor bear
the speaking of their name in our hearing.

Someone to Bleed on

The scribes and the Pharisees brought a woman who had been caught in adultery, and placing her in the midst they said to [Jesus], 'Teacher, this woman has been caught in the act of adultery. Now in the law Moses commanded us to stone such. What do you say about her?' This they said to test him, that they might have some charge to bring against him. Jesus bent down and wrote with his finger on the ground. And as they continued to ask him, he stood up and said to them, 'Let him who is without sin among you be the first to throw a stone at her.'

The story of the woman caught in adultery reads like something out of John Le Carré and the former East Germany's dirty tricks department. The scribes and the Pharisees haul the poor woman out in public, and encircle her like a trapped animal in a pit. They plan to use her as bait against Jesus.

Instinctively, we want to condemn them for ganging-up on this lone woman, for hemming her in like a pack of wolves, for their self-righteousness and nauseous moral superiority, and for their attempt to corner Jesus and put him on the spot in front of the people. They ask him, 'What do you say about her?'

What can he say about her? If he answers that she should be stoned to death in accordance with the law of Moses (Lev 20:10), then he is no friend of poor sinners. If he says she should not be stoned, then he is teaching contrary to the law of Moses – the law of God. Either way he's in their trap.

We notice that there is no mention of the man in the equation, the man who is the poor woman's accomplice in the act of adultery. Given the tenor of the times back then we should not expect there to be. Religion was a man's world until Jesus came into religious history.

Faced with the woman's entrapment and his own, Our Lord begins to do something strange. He starts writing on the ground with his finger. What was he writing? No one knows. But there are suggestions. Perhaps he was writing down the secret sins of the men in front of him. If he was doing this, we may assume he did it in a way that made each man's sins manifest only to that man himself. Barclay suggests that Jesus wrote to no particular purpose. Writing was merely his way of turning his face away from the 'bleak cruelty' of the crowd. James McPolin, in his commentary, thinks that the Lord's action may have been 'a studied refusal to pronounce judgement'. Perhaps the Lord just doodled, as though rating the accusers' spirit of religion and charity a great big zero.

When the pack of men persist in hassling Jesus he stands up and challenges them. He says, 'Let him who is without sin among you be the first to throw a stone at her.' No one casts a stone, for none of them is sinless. When it comes to a specific individual's behaviour, you and I should not be that person's judge. The qualification for judging, as Barclay wisely points out, is not our knowledge about someone but our own personal achievement in goodness. All of us are lacking in that domain. Therefore, only God may judge the individual's heart, motives and circumstances. The encircling men cannot, of course, cast a stone at the woman because they are all sinners. They know it and, I suspect, they realise that Jesus knows it too. That brings us to one of the most sobering lines in the entire Bible: 'They began to drift away beginning even with the eldest.'

The woman and Jesus are left alone, the sinner and the sinless One; or as St Augustine put it, 'there remained only a great misery and a great pity.' By pity, Augustine means kindness. Our Lord tells the woman that he is not going to condemn her. Instead, she has the chance to put her past behind her and start afresh. So he says to her, 'Go, and from now on, sin no more.'

You and I, dear people, must not judge others whose story is known only to themselves and to God. We lack sufficient moral achievement and holiness ourselves to be the moral judges of others. And there is – inevitably – the loss of our sense of justice and charity when we enter the group, or the club, or the mob and let others lead us by the nose. There is the lesson here that none of us is without sin and that each of us has to stand, at one time or another in our lives, as misery in the presence of pity. 'We all need someone we can bleed on,' sang Mick Jagger a few years ago in *Let it Bleed*. How true! The someone to bleed on is Jesus, as the woman in today's story was so fortunate to discover.

A Lesson from Pilate

Pilate then called together the chief priests and the rulers and the people, and said to them, 'You brought me this man as one who was perverting the people; and after examining him before you, behold, I did not find this man guilty of any of your charges against him; neither did Herod, for he sent him back to us. Behold, nothing deserving death has been done by him; I will therefore chastise him and release him.' But they all cried out together, 'Away with this man, and release to us Barabbas ...'

Pilate addressed them once more, desiring to release Jesus; but they shouted out, 'Crucify, crucify him!' A third time he said to them, 'Why, what evil has he done? I have found in him no crime deserving death; I will therefore chastise him and release him.' But they were urgent, demanding with loud cries that he should be crucified. And their voices prevailed. So Pilate gave sentence that their demand should be granted.

In the movie *Patton*, George C. Scott comes across as everybody's image of what the great wartime commander looked like. He is tough, square-jawed, built like a tank, and with a gravel voice to match. The truth is that the screen image of Patton doesn't match the real life Patton in much other than his vanity and battlefield successes.

In Franco Zeffirelli's *Jesus of Nazareth*, Rod Steiger comes across as most people's version of Pilate. He is the tough military commander sent as the no-nonsense Roman governor to a part of the empire that is forever bubbling over with arcane theology, Messianic expectations, sun-crazed zealots and insurrections. Pilate's job is to keep the lid firmly on this bubbling pot, and Rod Steiger is the man to do it! The truth is that the real life vacillating Pilate was not quite Hollywood's emphatic Rod Steiger.

The real life Pilate wished to set Jesus free but he hadn't the guts to do it. He was coerced by the crowd. In her private vision, *The Dolorous Passion*, Anne Catherine Emmerich portrays Pilate as a man who felt that Jesus should be freed as a matter of Roman justice. But he was a weak man. He had an empire behind him and yet was not able to withstand the pressure of the

43

rabble. So 'Pilate at last yielded,' says Emmerich. Barclay sees it
a little differently. Pilate yielded, he says, because he was a highly
compromised man, and it was Pilate's compromised status that
doomed Jesus.

The things compromising Pilate were all in his recent past.
On his appointment as governor his troops entered Jerusalem,
the holy city, with their Roman standards topped by the graven
image of the emperor-god. This insulted the Jews. Then he built
a new water system for the city but financed it with money taken
from the temple treasury. This inflamed the Jews. These may
have been the actions of a no-nonsense military commander but
they were not the actions of a prudent Roman governor. They
were grounds for civil incompetence and for dismissal.

Apparently, the Jews had not thus far made an official complaint to Rome about these insults, but there was always the
chance that they might. These were the things hanging over
Pilate's head and compromising him in his conduct of the trial of
Jesus. In Barclay's view, the crowd hints at the threat of complaint when they say to Pilate, 'If you release this man you are
not the friend of Caesar.' (Jn 19:12) It meant, 'We may report the
things you did if you release this man, and then you will no
longer be part of the emperor's official family [called "the
friends of Caesar"], for you will be dismissed.'

Barclay says, '[Pilate] sacrificed justice rather than lose his
post ... Had he been a man of real courage he would have done
the right and taken the consequences, but his past made him a
coward.'

We are disgusted by Pilate's lack of guts, of course, but
would we behave better in a similar situation? Or would we too
sacrifice justice and the truth in order to hang on to our jobs?
Would we, as clergy, risk our positions in the church, or, as laity,
in the company, or in the government? Would we risk our
standing in the community? Each of us has to answer such questions for ourselves. It is clear enough from our recent social and
religious history that there are people who would sacrifice justice and truth for the sake of their skins, and have done so. Pilate
is no lone figure in any institution's history book.

Let the tragedy of Pilate's moral cowardice, and what it did
to Jesus, encourage you and me to develop in ourselves a finely
tuned sense of truth and justice and fair play in regard to our
neighbours' reputations, rights and lives.

Love as Service

Jesus ... rose from supper, laid aside his garments, and girded himself with a towel. Then he poured water into a basin, and began to wash his disciples' feet, and to wipe them with the towel ... He came to Simon Peter; and Peter said to him, 'Lord, are you going to wash my feet?' Jesus answered him, 'What I am doing you do not know now, but afterward you will understand.' Peter said to him, 'You shall never wash my feet.' Jesus answered him, 'If I do not wash you, you have no part in me.' Simon Peter said to him, 'Lord, then not my feet only but also my hands and my head!' When he had washed their feet, and taken his garments, and resumed his place, he said to them, 'Do you understand what I have done for you?'

A bank I did business with had a slogan: 'Service is our most important product.' That line ought to be a golden rule among Christians. It was a golden rule with Jesus.

In the gospel we've just heard Jesus is having his farewell supper with his friends. On the religious level, he is celebrating Passover with his disciples, and he is about to institute the momentous ritual that we call the Mass. On the personal level, he is about to pass from this world to the Father. At this critical time, when he should be absorbed in these matters, what does he do? He starts washing feet!

Washing feet has no apparent relationship with what has been unfolding thus far in the Passover meal and the farewell supper. It comes as an about-face, something entirely unexpected. But, obviously, Jesus knew what he was doing. He intended this unusual incident, and he intended it to underline dramatically a critical Christian teaching. It is this: service is our most important product. Service is the expression of the commandment of love. A Christian is defined by service.

Our Lord teaches by doing. He picks up the basin. He pours water into it. He bends down each time, passing from one disciple to the other. He does the washing. He does the drying. There is no pious pep talk here, nor stylised liturgical ritual. Our Lord's actions are his words. When he finishes he asks, 'Do you understand what I have just done? If I, whom you call Lord and Master, wash your feet, you must do likewise for one another.' If we do not understand the centrality of loving service in the life of the Christian then 'you can have no part with me.'

Our own lives, to the contrary, are full of scrambling for recognition and for the position and the status that require others to serve us. We are miffed when others do not give us the deference due our titles, or the place of honour our dignity assumes it deserves. We are in love with the pecking order syndrome. It infects government and big business and even the small office we work in. It infects the church, for all its talk and documents to the contrary. William Barclay comments: 'Here [in this gospel scene] is the lesson that there is only one kind of greatness, the greatness of service. The world is full of people who are standing on their dignity when they ought to be kneeling at the feet of their brethren.'

Let us not hear these words, nod our heads in pious agreement, and go away saying, 'What a lovely thought!' Let us believe the lovely thought in the way Jesus believed it – by doing it – as he, our Lord and Master, did as an example for us.

Keepers of the Dreaming

Now on the first day of the week Mary Magdalene came to the tomb early, while it was still dark, and saw that the stone had been taken away from the tomb. So she ran, and went to Simon Peter and the other disciple, the one whom Jesus loved, and said to them, 'They have taken the Lord out of the tomb, and we do not know where they have laid him.' Peter then came out with the other disciple, and they went toward the tomb ... and stooping to look in, [they] saw the linen cloths lying there ...

Morris West relates this incident in his book, *A View From The Ridge.* He was in the town of Alice Springs in Northern Australia prior to the Pope's visit in 1986. A community of very poor Aboriginal people lived on the edge of the town. They were called the fringe dwellers.

They lived in government housing, had little or no work, and declined under 'the white man's curse of alcohol'. The men spent their idle days in what passed for their meeting houses on the dry bed of the river, their refuse heaps everywhere: piles of beer cans and broken bottles. It was a depressing sight. West wondered if there was anything positive he could write about 'these lost people.'

That night the parish priest took him to the schoolhouse. There was someone the priest wanted West to meet. The some-one was a tall Aborigine man. He was painting a canvas. The canvas would form the backdrop of the altar for the Pope's Mass. The man was painting the tribal history of his people on this canvas, all forty thousand years of it! The priest said to West, 'That man is a very special person. His people have no written language. All their history is orally transmitted. All of it is locked inside the head of that man. He is the Keeper of the Dreaming for all his people.'

Then it struck West that the man who was coming, the Pope from Rome, was also a keeper of a dreaming. He was a keeper of a two-thousand-year dreaming. It was the dreaming, and the role of the keeper of the dreaming, that connected two very dif-ferent men and cultures, and gave West something to write about.

Today's gospel on the resurrection must remind us, dear friends, that we too are the keepers of a dreaming. We are the keepers of the Christian dreaming. The Christian dreaming is the story of our salvation through Christ's passion, death and resurrection with its promise of glory.

The dreaming is the story of each Christian generation, and ourselves now, rising from the tomb of sin and living the new life of grace in Christ. And it is the story of each Christian generation, and ourselves now, establishing the kingdom of God on earth and facing the future with confidence and full of the hope of glory. For such is the promise of him who went to glory ahead of us. The Lord's resurrection today is proof that there is power to the promise he made when he said, 'I go to prepare a place for you, and then I shall come back to take you with me, that where I am you also may be. You know the way that leads to where I go ... I am the way.' (Jn 14: 2-3)

We are the keepers of this Christian dreaming, and we are its transmitters. The dreaming came to us from those who went before us, and we are charged with passing it on to those who follow us. When Jesus had completed his mission he said to his disciples, 'Go into the whole world and proclaim the good news to everyone.' (Mk 16:15) From that day to this, the Christian generations have been the keepers of his dreaming, and they have transmitted it faithfully, else we would not be its possessors now. We are the present link in the chain of the dreaming.

May you have, then, a happy Easter. May you feel assured in your faith that your Lord has risen as he said he would. May your every day be glad with the expectation of your own glory to come. May you experience the inner peace of those who keep and transmit the Christian dreaming, those who are the keepers and the transmitters of his marvellous story and of its saving promises in their regard.

The Church's Charter

On the evening of that day, the first day of the week, the doors being shut where the disciples were, for fear of the Jews, Jesus came and stood among them and said to them, 'Peace be with you.' When he had said this, he showed them his hands and his side. Then the disciples were glad when they saw the Lord. Jesus said to them again, 'Peace be with you. As the Father has sent me, even so I send you.' And when he had said this, he breathed on them, and said to them, 'Receive the Holy Spirit. If you forgive the sins of any, they are forgiven; if you retain the sins of any, they are retained.'

There is a contrast in today's gospel. Contrasted are the fear of the disciples and the confidence of the risen Lord. The disciples are locked in the room for fear of the Jews. Their Lord has been taken and killed, and it may be their turn next. They believe that their Lord is still locked in his tomb, and it is now the third day, and there is no rumour of his resurrection. They fear they have no future.

Then the risen Lord appears to them and their fearfulness changes to confidence. He says, 'Peace be with you.' His greeting is not just a wish or a hope. It is a statement. It does not mean, may peace be with you. It means peace is with you. The presence of the Lord, in the power of his resurrection, enables that peace to be with them. Its effect is shown in their rejoicing.

The Lord then endows them with his own mission. He passes on to them the mission that was given him by the Father. He breathes the commissioning Spirit on them as the God of Genesis breathed life into Adam and as the God of Ezekiel harnessed the wind to breathe new life into the dead bodies of Israel in the valley of the dry bones. (Ezek 37:9) The church sees in this commissioning of the disciples its own commissioning to the mission and ministry of Christ.

It also sees the granting of its charter. The charter is the rights and obligations relative to the mission of Jesus and the preaching of the gospel. Down the generations the church, as institution, has been conscious of the rights but, perhaps, not always equally conscious of the obligations. The church is always in danger of stressing its authority more than its obligations of ser-

vice, its rights more than its heart in the interpretation of the
Lord's word and its loving intent. The church is always in danger of substituting its own word for his, itself for him, forgetting
that it is not Christ but his spiritual body. It not the Bridegroom,
as St Paul said, but the spotted bride. (Eph 5:27) Barclay, with
good servant sense, stresses the obligations of the church's charter over its rights. For the church is chartered mainly, he says, to
be 'the mouth to speak for Jesus, feet to run upon his errands,
hands to do his work'.

Among the rights of the charter is a quite awesome one. The
church has the right and the power to forgive or retain sins.
Some Christian churches understand this as the church's ability
to declare a person justified before God. Our own church exer-
cises the power in several ways but especially through sacramental absolution. Perhaps the issue of how this power of forgiveness is correctly exercised, whether by declaration or by
absolution, should not be the primary concern of the churches
but rather why so few people today wish to be declared just or
experience sacramental forgiveness.

Let us pray today for the church in its mission. Let us retain
our faith in the church, at a difficult time, as the body chartered
and missioned by the Lord. And let us pray for a sharper sense
of our own personal sinfulness and our more frequent use of the
sacrament of reconciliation. Above all, let us pray for a better
sense of ourselves, unworthy though we be, as the church and as
its missionaries no matter to what seemingly small degree.

Tending our Time

Just as day was breaking, Jesus stood on the beach; yet the disciples did not know that it was Jesus. Jesus said to them, 'Children, have you any fish?' They answered him, 'No.' He said to them, 'Cast the net on the right side of the boat, and you will find some.' So they cast it, and now they were not able to haul it in, for the quantity of fish.

The prophet Ezekiel lived during the exile of the Jewish people in Babylon. In his prophecy he quotes a proverb often on the lips of the exiles, 'The fathers have eaten green grapes, and their children's teeth are on edge.' (Ezek 18:2) By this proverb, the exiles meant to blame their lamentable state on the Jewish generations that went before them. Those generations had not lived up to God's law and had not taught their children to live by God's law; hence the exile to Babylon and the dire straits the exiles now found themselves in.

One generation is responsible to a significant degree for the next generation, and the exiles in Babylon would be the first to agree. The torch is passed on, as JFK said, 'to a new generation'. (Inaugural Address, 20/1/1961) The torch is the culture, the values, and the vision of a people. There is no guarantee, of course, that the new generation appreciates what is passed on, and that it will choose to live by its light. But, at least, it is given light for the start of its journey in history. From then on it must plough its own furrow and light its own way. If it opts for darkness, or for a different light down the road, that's its responsibility.

Today's gospel is about passing on the torch. Jesus is the light of the world and his words and values are its rays. It is his hope that all the peoples of the earth will be gathered to him. He makes his disciples central to this work. He comes upon them in the early morning by the lakeside. They do not recognise him, possibly because the light is poor in the morning or, more likely, because his appearance is changed due to the resurrection. The disciples have been fishing all night and have caught nothing. Jesus speaks to them in what James McPolin calls a familiar and colloquial tone, 'Lads, you haven't caught anything, have you?' They still do not recognise him, except for John. Jesus tells them to cast the net again. They do so, and the net is filled with large fish. John even tells us how many: one hundred and fifty three.

Since John is the theologian of sign and symbol there must be a reason why he noted the number 153. Was there a popular belief in his time, handed down from generation to generation, that 153 was the number of the different species of fish that God created in the beginning? And did St Jerome, in his commentary, assume that when John mentioned 153 he was using it to symbolise all the peoples of the earth who would be gathered into the church by those whom Jesus makes 'fishers of men'? (Mk 1:17)

The bulging net not torn symbolises the ingathering of huge numbers, and the fact that none destined for salvation shall be lost. It suggests that the gospel is open to everyone irrespective of economics, culture, colour, ethnicity, social status and sex. As Paul will say later of the church, 'There no longer exists among you Jew or Greek, slave or freeman, male or female. All are one in Christ Jesus.' (Gal 3:28)

One lesson we learn from today's gospel is the reality of the Lord's resurrection and his visible, if changed, appearance to the disciples. We are being told that the Lord's resurrection and our faith do not rest on fiction or on faith only, but on fact. It is a lesson that should strengthen our faith and the faith of the generation that follows us.

A second lesson is the lesson of the bulging net. Our Lord expects the whole world to come to him and to live by his light. His expectation is not a self-serving one: it is a matter of his Father's will and humankind's need. It is for this that he called the first disciples and made them 'fishers of men' in their time. He has chosen you and me to be among the fishers of our time. The bulging net is as much a challenge to us as it was to apostles. Let us do our best, then, in both passing on the torch and casting the net.

Bonds of Love

[Jesus said], 'My sheep hear my voice, and I know them, and they follow me; and I give them eternal life, and they shall never perish, and no one shall snatch them out of my hand. My Father, who has given them to me, is greater than all, and no one is able to snatch them out of the Father's hand. I and the Father are one.'

No government has ever been elected by a unanimous vote in a democracy. Many governments have been given large majorities, of course, and even landslide victories but a unanimous vote among millions of free voters is too much to expect in a healthy democracy. That degree of unanimity, someone has said, is only found in cemeteries.

In today's gospel, Jesus speaks of unanimity. He speaks of the oneness of mind and heart between his Father and himself. There is an unbreakable bond of love between them. Then he speaks of the bond between himself and his flock. So strong is this bond that no one shall be able to snatch his beloved flock away from him.

We must, then, matter immensely to Jesus. The gospel's repeated lines about the shepherd and his flock, and the bonding love of the two, are almost beyond the scripture's ability with words. We are the Father's flock. He has given the flock to Jesus. We are become Jesus' flock. We are always on his mind. We are always in his heart. He is always calling to us. He knows us by name. He prays that not a single one of us, whom the Father has given him, shall ever be lost. He has, even now, gone to prepare a place for us so that when our time is done we will be at his side for eternity.

At the Last Supper, in page after page of John's gospel, Jesus tells his disciples that the core of his message is love. Love must also be the core of our Christian lives. It must define us. We are not talking here about any old kind of love. We are talking about loving each other as he has loved us. (cf Jn 15:12) Jesus said, 'I give you a new commandment: love one another. Such as my love has been for you, so must your love be for one another. This is how all will know you for my disciples: your love for one another.' (Jn 13:34-35 [NAB])

Some of us, perhaps, may feel overly challenged by the cali-bre of the love Jesus expects of us. He asks us to love one another as he has loved us. That seems to stretch our capacity beyond its limits. We are tempted to revert to the view held by various crit-ics throughout history that such love is a chimera in a world which is naturally violent, and that if Christians actually prac-tised Christ's selfless love they would be as lambs to the slaugh-ter. Is that not what happened to Christ himself? But to say such things is to presume that Christian love is purely passive. It is not. It can be as tough as it can be tender, and sometimes must be. Pope Paul VI made some provocative comments on the stronger side of Christian love, and we do well to listen to them.

He said, in his Address of 27/1/1971, that we are familiar with the loving Christ who is poor and meek. And we are famil-iar with the Christ who submits to violence, who turns the other cheek, and who was led like a lamb to the slaughter. But there is another Christ, he says, and another form of his love. It is still the same loving Christ but this time it is the strong Christ, the polemical Christ, the reforming Christ, the Christ of contestation and anathema. This is the 'virile and severe' Christ, said the Pope, even the 'indignant and pugnacious' Christ. And, he added, in regard to Christ's tough love, we should consider the 'reforming energy' which Christ brought to bear on 'this fallen and corrupt world.' In other words, Christ's love was as con-frontational at times as it was meek at times, everything depend-ing on the circumstances at hand. Yet, either way, Christ's love was a selfless and an others-serving love.

Paul VI hoped that we would bring a strong love, a challeng-ing, prophetic and reforming love to bear in rearing our families amid negative peer pressure and in the face of neighbourhood disvalues; that we would bring such a love to bear when con-versing with our lax friends, in our involvement in civic affairs, when confronting social evils, and when contesting for social values. A prophetic and a contesting and a tough love, not a meek love, is called for in many instances in the living of the true Christian life. This, then, is the other side of love, its toughness. It is love with a backbone. It was intimated by Jesus when he said, 'I am come to light a fire on the earth; how I wish the blaze were ignited!' (Lk 12:49) and when he said, 'I have come to bring not peace but the sword.' (Mt 10:34)

It is fitting that we who are the Shepherd's flock should do

our best to love as he loved. Most often our love will be the love
that is as gentle as a mother's love, but sometimes it must be love
in the image of the biblical refiner with the flaming fire, the fire
that burns, though burning only to separate the dross from the
gold.

Loving as He Loved Us

[Jesus said], 'A new commandment I give to you, that you love one another; even as I have loved you, that you also love one another. By this all men will know that you are my disciples, if you have love for one another.'

Gabriel Garcia Marquez is a Columbian writer who won the Nobel Prize for literature in 1982. His stories are human and humorous, a little odd to the Western mind maybe, and perhaps even a bit surreal. Accordingly, his story entitled 'The Saint' (in *Strange Pilgrims*) might not fit our notion of sanctity, of what it is that makes a saint.

The story is about a man named Margarito. His wife died in the birth of their only child. Then the child, a girl, died at the age of seven. Eleven years later, when the village cemetery was being moved to make way for a dam, the child's body was found to be incorrupt. More surprisingly, it was found to be weightless. Since incorruptibility is a possible sign of sanctity the whole nation got behind Margarito and the cause of his little girl's canonisation. Margarito went off to Rome to push the cause, and brought the weightless body of 'the saint' with him. There our author met him for the first time. But all of Margarito's efforts to get anyone in officialdom to take his weightless 'saint' seriously were to no avail. Yet he persisted with his faith and in his love year in and year out.

Our author returned to Rome twenty-two years after he first met Margarito, and perhaps he would not have thought about him at all if they had not run into each other by accident. One day a voice that might have come from the beyond stopped him in the street. It was Margarito. He had grown old and tired but was still waiting for someone in the official church to listen to the cause of his weightless 'saint'. Our author writes: 'Four popes had died ... and still he waited. "I've waited so long it can't be much longer now," he told me as he said goodbye ... He shuffled down the middle of the street, wearing the combat boots and faded cap of an old Roman, ignoring the puddles of rain where the light was beginning to decay. Then I had no doubt, if I ever had any at all, that the saint was Margarito.

Without realising it, by means of his daughter's incorruptible body and while he was still alive, he had spent twenty-two years fighting for the legitimate cause of his own canonisation.'

If Margarito is a saint, as our author believed him to be, he is a saint of love. Love more than nature compelled him. The years of waiting for an official ear to hear him pass by, and they gather like old swept leaves in the corner of a Roman street. The story ends with this image of a father grown old under the weight of his mission and under the weight of his love. Margarito, not his weightless child, is the real saint in the story.

Jesus commanded his disciples to love. But it's not the usual limited forms of love that he had in mind. He said, 'Love one another as I have loved you.' The effect of loving one another as he has loved us is that 'all people will know that you are my disciples.' You and I look at the North, or at the war history of Europe, or at the divisions in Christian history, or at the factions in our own church today. Do these things suggest that Christians have been, and still are, in love with each other? Or are they are principally in love with their own particular version of church, with their private theologies, with their particular take on things? Yet loving one another, and loving one another to the depth that Jesus loved us, is the church. Nothing else adequately defines church. And we should stop trying to make other things define what church properly is and what church properly does.

The love that Jesus wants from us is true and deep and it is costly. Jean Anouilh says, 'Love is, above all, the gift of oneself.' (*Ardèle*) Our Lord gave himself in life and death for us. And when we left Margarito at the start of the twenty-third year of his self-imposed exile in Rome, he was still making its streets holy under his shuffling and ageing and ever-loving feet.

Be Not Afraid!

[Jesus said], 'These things I have spoken to you, while I am still with you. But the Counsellor, the Holy Spirit, whom the Father will send in my name, he will teach you all things, and bring to your remembrance all that I have said to you ... Let not your hearts be troubled, neither let them be afraid.'

After the Second World War the Swiss physician, Paul Tournier, wrote a little book on the fragmentation of modern life. It was published in English as *The Whole Person in a Broken World*. Its thesis is simple: post-war Western society has no room for God; in 'killing-off' God it is destroying itself, for its foundations are spiritual and its mortar mainly Christian. How can it expect to survive in decent shape without them? Is it for the same reason that the Holy Father, and many of us, support the new Europe but worry about its excessive secularisation and its drift from God?

Tournier saw much fragmentation in people's lives. He found many of his patients trying to live their lives without God. It wasn't working. Some of us suspect that we see the same fragmentation in our new society.

The church too seems fragmented. We have our camps and our cliques which separate along doctrinal and ethical fracture lines. And there is more than a small measure of anxiety and confusion in church leadership and in the rank-and-file. 'There is no peace even in the church. It is rent by tensions,' says St Josemaria Escriva forthrightly in *Christ Is Passing By*. The gospel today may well be speaking to all of these forms of fragmentation.

Jesus tells us that he and the Father will send the Holy Spirit to be our counsellor. We certainly need one. A counsellor is an advocate. He is someone who takes up our cause and who defends us and fights for us. James McPolin, in his commentary, calls the Spirit 'a helper in faith.' The Holy Spirit helps believers when they sincerely seek his help. Do we, as individuals and as church, too readily presume rather than plead the Spirit's assistance? The years of child abuse seem to answer, yes. As our helper in faith the Spirit helps us to understand the teachings of

Jesus, to uncover them with a deeper spiritual insight, and to clothe ourselves in ministry with them. But this multi-layered assistance from the Spirit presupposes genuine interest, study and pleading prayer on our part.

William Barclay, in his commentary, calls the Holy Spirit 'an ally'. The Spirit was Jesus' ally in his agony and death. As an ally, the Spirit did not help Jesus avoid suffering and death, but saw him faithfully through them. The Spirit is now our ally in the agony of life and in the trouble and turmoil of these end times. The Spirit will not help us avoid these but will see us, as true believers, safely through them.

I sometimes wonder if some of our contemporary visionaries and message bearers are not too heavy on the threats and the chastisements, and too light on the gospel of Christ with its assurance of the Counsellor-Ally sent to assist true believers and to light their way. The crucial issue here is whether we, as church and as individuals, are true believers. Do we seek the Spirit's guidance sufficiently? Do we really ask for it? Notice Jesus! 'I will ask the Father and he will give you another Paraclete to be with you always.' (Jn 14:16) 'If you, with all your sins, know how to give your children good things, how much more will the heavenly Father give the Holy Spirit to those who ask him.' (Lk 11:13)

Our Lord tells us not to be afraid, not to be anxious, in this time of his absence. There is no need for fear and anxiety with the Spirit helping us and counselling us. In addition to the Spirit, Jesus gives us his gift of peace for this time of his absence. It fills the heart of the true believer with the inner peace, the integrating peace, that Tournier found lacking in his patients. It is the peace promised for the age of the Messiah. It is deep-down joy in the knowledge of one's salvation and in the assurance of one's glory.

Barclay writes, 'No experience of life can ever take [Christ's peace] from us and no sorrow, no danger, no suffering can ever make it less.' There is no reason, then, for us to be anxious or afraid or fragmented in the time of the Lord's absence. We have the Holy Spirit for our helper, and the peace of the Lord Jesus at the core of ourselves, while we await his coming again in glory.

The Way to Go

Then [Jesus] opened their minds to understand the scriptures, and said to them, 'Thus it is written, that the Christ should suffer and on the third day rise from the dead, and that repentance and forgiveness of sins should be preached in his name to all nations, beginning from Jerusalem ...' Then he led them out as far as Bethany, and lifting up his hands he blessed them. While he blessed them, he parted from them, and was carried up into heaven.

Death disturbs us. We do not like to think about it. It is something we wish to delay as long as possible. 'To evade death is one of the oldest and strongest desires of rulers,' writes Nobel Prize winner Elias Canetti in his study of mass psychology, *Crowds And Power*. Canetti's line can be applied to all of us and not just to our leaders. One of humanity's oldest and strongest desires is to evade death. The Welsh poet Dylan Thomas wrote, of the dying of his father, 'Do not go gentle into that good night./ Rage, rage against the dying of the light.' (*Do Not Go Gentle Into That Good Night*)

I think it fair to say that Western society is in a state of denial with regard to death. Now that is not to say that we are purely escapists, or that prior generations liked death more than we do. But they didn't try to deny it as we do. However unlovable and unwanted, they faced it realistically and accepted it as a plain fact of life. Life for them was short and harsh even at the best of times and, if I may use an oxymoron, death was a reality that lived in their houses.

In recent years, psychology has addressed the issue of the denial of death. Ernest Becker wrote a seminal work on the subject in 1972 appropriately titled, *The Denial Of Death*. Elisabeth Kübler-Ross in 1969 charted the stages we go through, as dying persons, moving from denial to acceptance. (*On Death And Dying*) In her counselling and in her writings she gives us the view of death as a 'friendly passage'. For example, many near-death experiences record the person entering an arena of soft light or emerging from a tunnel into friendly light to be met by God or by loved ones.

Good Pope John XXIII expressed a confident acceptance of

death when, a few days before his own, he reportedly said, 'I am able to follow my own death step by step. Now I move softly towards the end.'

Nowhere will one find so calming a view of death as the Christian one which we celebrate today, viz. death as ascension to the Father. Jesus, our model and the pattern of our Christian lives, ascends into heaven. He ascends to much more than soft light and friendly passage: he ascends to glory. Glory is our assured and blessed future in Christ. The ascension of the Lord is the final phase in Christ's victory over death. That is why Paul writes, 'Christ, once raised from the dead, will never die again; death has no more power over him.' (Rom 6:9) Death has no lasting power over Christ, and it has no lasting power over the Christian believer. Our destiny is not the grave, but glory.

Death, then, is not terminal. Death does not end us. It doesn't erase us. It cannot consign us to the grave and to insignificance and to nothing more. Our Lord's ascension is prototype and power of our own.

Today's feast, then, is a theology of hope for you and for me, for the young and the old, for the apprehensive and the accepting, for those who mourn and for those who deny. Be assured that Our Lord ascended into glory and that we, being faithful, shall do the same.

A Prayer for the Church

[Jesus said], 'I do not pray for these [disciples] only, but also for those who believe in me through their word, that they may all be one; even as you, Father, are in me, and I in you, that they also may be in us, so that the world may believe that you sent me.'

Today's gospel forms the final part of Jesus' prayer to his Father for his disciples. He prays that they may be one as he and the Father are one. Then he prays for all the people who, through their word, will come to believe in him. He prays that these people also will be one with him and his Father, and one in a communion of mind and heart together. Jesus is praying for the church. He is praying for the church of the apostles, the first generation church, and he is praying for the church of all the generations. And we, the church of today, are included in his prayer.

The unity that Jesus prays for his church is above all the unity of love. Nothing so defines the church of Jesus as love. Every other definition of church is secondary. At various times in the church's history it has put the emphasis in the wrong place. Jesus said, 'I give you a new commandment: love one another. Such as my love has been for you, so must your love be for each other. This is how all will know you for my disciples: your love for one another.' (Jn 13:34-35 NAB) Henry Chadwick says of the great growth of the post-apostolic church: 'The practical application of love was probably the most potent single cause of Christian success.' (*The Early Church*)

Have we forgotten – not in our official documents but in our performance – that love defines the true church? The victims of child sexual abuse, for example, say that the institutional church of our time has defined itself by canon law and cover-up rather than by love, that it has ruled by stealth rather than by pastoral concern.

'Love has been lost to us,' claims Morris West in *A View From The Ridge*. He names himself as a victim of unloving church laws and unjust church processes. His is 'the testimony of an ageing pilgrim, one of the elders who has been a long time on the road'. Authority in the church, he says, is 'a one-eyed man' in the absence of love. 'The fact is we can live only in communion.' In our day, and for the future, we badly need a 'curative communion' in our church. Only the primacy of love can deliver that curative communion.

Barclay's says that the unity Jesus prayed for was not unity under authority, or unity of administration, or unity of organisation – the unity that church leadership *de facto* prioritises. What Jesus prayed for was the unity of loving relationship. 'We have already seen [in the gospel] that the union between Jesus and God was one of love and obedience. It was a unity of love for which Jesus prayed, a unity in which men loved each other because they loved him, a unity based entirely on the relationship between heart and heart.'

Let us pray for the primacy of love and for the primacy of the unity of love in our church. Let us pray that the Spirit Jesus sent will bind us together in such love. Let us pray that we will be open to receive unifying love, and to give it. There is no other cure for the hurt among us in the wake of the abuse and the victimisation, the cover-up and the neglect. No new canon law or talk of 'zero tolerance' can ever take the place of love, or be as effective as love. We, in the church, need to face the fact that the growth of law is only the sign of the absence of love. Nothing substitutes for love. We simply are not Christ's church without it.

St John of the Cross' summation of the Christian life still holds true: 'In the evening of life we shall be judged on our love.' How the Lord originally defined his church also still holds true, and always will. 'Love one another. Such as my love has been for you, so must your love be for each other. This is how all will know you for my disciples: your love for one another.' (Jn 13: 34-35)

Pentecost: Gospel: Jn 20:19-23

We are God's Helpers

Jesus came and stood among them and said to them, 'Peace be with you.' When he had said this, he showed them his hands and his side. Then the disciples were glad when they saw the Lord. Jesus said to them again, 'Peace be with you. As the Father has sent me, even so I send you.' And when he had said this, he breathed on them, and said to them, 'Receive the Holy Spirit. If you forgive the sins of any, they are forgiven; if you retain the sins of any, they are retained.'

You may recall, dear friends, hearing this gospel passage as part of the gospel reading for the 2nd Sunday of Easter. The heart of this gospel is the so-called commissioning of the church by Jesus, the commission to carry on his mission. He said to the disciples, 'As the Father has sent me, even so I send you.'

The church as we normally understand it, as it is structured today, did not exist when Jesus spoke these words of commissioning. So the trouble with any talk about the commissioning of 'the church' is that we tend to think of the church in its institutional form and, therefore, in limited form. We think of Rome. We think of the Pope and the bishops and the priests. We see them as the church and as the ones Jesus is commissioning today. We do not think of the laity as the church. We do not think of ourselves as commissioned by Jesus to carry on his mission. But we are.

A cherished task of mine for twenty-one years was preparing men and women for missionary work abroad. They served in such places as Malawi, Ghana, Samoa and New Guinea as catechists, school teachers, doctors, nurses, mission supply pilots, mechanics, masons, agricultural advisors, etc. They signed for two- and three-year terms which were renewable after evaluation. I eventually had to give up this work because of the pressure of other assignments. On leaving, they asked me to name my parting gift. I asked for the same ring which they received from the cardinal at their commissioning ceremony. It was a plain gold band with the inscription, 'For we are God's helpers.' These words are a compression of several scriptures calling all of us to service and to ministry.

For we are God's helpers. All of us are. The church is not just

64

the Pope and the bishops and the priests and the deacons. The church is the whole People of God. The People of God are 'a people God acquired for himself' (*Catechism of the Catholic Church*, #782), 'a chosen race, a royal priesthood, a holy nation.' (1 Pet 2:9) The mission of this people, says the *Catechism*, is to be 'the salt of the earth and the light of the world' (cf Mt 5:13-16) and to be 'a most sure seed of unity, hope and salvation for the whole human race'.

All of us, continues the *Catechism*, share the prophetic office of the church. The prophetic office involves adhering to our faith, deepening our understanding and appreciation of it, and being Christ's witnesses in the midst of the world (#785). In other words, we are both the church and its missionaries.

Chiara Lubich, who founded the Focolare movement, writes, 'One thing is certain. Our world that is so wounded can only be healed by Jesus.' (*From Scripture To Life*) Now you and I are become Jesus' heart and voice and hands in our own time and place. He loves, speaks to, and lifts up others through us. St Josemaria Escriva, the advocate of lay holiness through ordinary daily life, writes, 'The work of salvation is still going on, and each one of us has a part in it.' (*Christ Is Passing By*)

We are God's helpers. We are his helpers in continuing the mission and the work he gave his Son and which the Son, in turn, gave us. We witness to Christ's cross by carrying our own with faith and in imitation of him. We witness to his resurrection by rising from our own sins and living in grace and goodness. We witness to the saving love of God, as Jesus did, by being the ambassadors of a love that is as selfless as possible in the service, the care, the compassion, and the healing of others.

What is Truth?

[Jesus said], 'When the Spirit of truth comes, he will guide you into all the truth; for he will not speak on his own authority, but whatever he hears he will speak, and he will declare to you the things that are to come. He will glorify me, for he will take what is mine and declare it to you. All that the Father has is mine; therefore I said that he will take what is mine and declare it to you.'

Today is the Feast of the Most Holy Trinity. The Trinity is called the fundamental mystery of Christianity. A mystery, in the religious sense, is something hidden. God is mystery because his nature is hidden insofar as our ability to know it is concerned. Our limited human nature needs the assistance of revelation to know God.

We know quite a bit about God due to revelation and especially due to what Jesus has disclosed about God. Yet there is much we shall not know until we meet God face to face in the openness of eternity. St Paul writes, 'Now we see in a mirror dimly, but then face to face. Now I know in part; then I shall understand fully.' (1 Cor 13:12)

Jesus, in particular, tells us that God is three divine Persons, Father, Son and Spirit. He tells us about their work. An important part of their work is bringing us God's truth. Jesus, as the Son of God, brings us the truth and the Holy Spirit confirms that truth in us.

At his trial Jesus said to Pilate, 'I have come into the world to bear witness to the truth.' Pilate asked him, 'What is truth?' (Jn 18:37-38) More than one critic has remarked that Jesus never answered Pilate's question. On the other hand, more than one critic has countered that Pilate did not wait to get the answer. In today's gospel, Jesus says, 'When the Spirit of truth comes, he will guide you into all the truth.' A major function of the Spirit, then, is to guide us to the fullness of the truth which Jesus bore witness to. The truth which Jesus bore witness to is, basically, three-fold. It is the truth about God, the truth that Jesus is God's faithful witness, and the truth about salvation.

Jesus reveals the true God to us. Before his coming most people worshipped idols. The chosen people alone knew God, but even they not fully. Today many people once again worship idols, even if these idols come in modern and more sophisticated forms. Jesus reveals the true God to us and teaches us how to worship God properly. He shows us how to relate with God. Jesus is God's faithful witness in these matters. He is, in fact, the one and only definitive witness.

Jesus teaches the truth about life and about ourselves. Life's meaning is the great question to which every generation seeks the answer. Jesus was sent by God to be 'the way and the truth' (Jn 14:6) by which this question is resolved. He was sent that we might not only understand the purpose of life but live it at a new level, the level of grace. You and I have accepted this grace and now we need to grow with it to what St Paul calls 'the measure of the stature of the fullness of Christ.' (Eph 4:13) This may be astounding to our minds, but it is entirely possible through Christ's elevating grace. Our great destiny is glory in heaven with God. Jesus teaches us – and anyone who will listen – that such is the truth about life and its meaning, about ourselves, our worth, our capability through grace, and our future.

All who follow Jesus become his disciples, the gathering of those who worship God 'in spirit and in truth.' (Jn 4:24) They allow the Spirit to transform them with the truth of Jesus. They allow the Spirit to lead them to ever deeper insight with regard to Christ's truth as guidance for their lives and for their future glory. When we invoke the enlightening Spirit he guides us in our prayers and in our spiritual progress. He guides us in our study of the word of God. He leads us to delight in God's word. He directs us in our vocations, our enterprises, our moral decisions and good works, and in the counselling of our children. Nothing is beyond the Holy Spirit's power to touch with grace, enlightenment, counsel, consolation and love.

Liturgy and Life

When the crowds learned [where Jesus was], they followed him; and he welcomed them and spoke to them of the kingdom of God, and cured those who had need of healing. Now the day began to wear away; and the twelve came and said to him, 'Send the crowd away, to go to the villages and the country round about, to lodge and get provisions; for we are here in a lonely place.' But he said to them, 'You give them something to eat.' They said, 'We have no more than five loaves and two fish – unless we are to go and buy food for all these people.'... And taking the five loaves and the two fish he looked up to heaven, and blessed and broke them, and gave them to the disciples to set before the crowd. And all ate and were satisfied. And they took up what was left over, twelve baskets of broken pieces.

One of the characters in Sean O'Casey's *The Plough and the Stars* says, 'There's no reason to bring religion into it. I think we ought to have as great a regard for religion as we can, so as to keep it out of as many things as possible.' I suspect that the years ahead in the new Ireland of the new Europe will see religion kept out of as many things as possible.

As I write Europe struggles over whether it should give God a mention in its proposed constitution. Religion is seen more and more as a private matter and a socially contentious subject and, perhaps, Europe may be inclined to buy O'Casey's point-of-view.

Religion is a private matter on one level, of course. But it has another level which is not private at all but eminently social. A good illustration of this two-tiered nature of religion is seen in today's gospel. Jesus and his disciples need a rest. They have been 'on tour' with the good news. As soon as they reach their proposed resting place they find the crowds already there. You and I might be upset over this unfair intrusion of the people but the gospel merely notes that Jesus 'welcomed' them. You and I might gripe about unfairness and the invasion of our privacy but Jesus sees the situation as human need, and he responds with compassion.

As the day draws to a close, the people are very hungry. The disciples alert Jesus to this fact. 'Send the crowds away,' they say to him, 'so they can get something to eat in the towns and villages.' Jesus says, 'You feed them.' The disciples are staggered at this. How can they possibly feed so many with only five loaves and two fish? Jesus multiplies the loaves and the fish so that all the people may eat. He involves the disciples in his feeding of the crowds. He gives them the food so they, in turn, may give it to the people. We learn from this scene that religion is not just a private matter but has a social dimension, and we learn that those who follow the Lord must not have idle but helping hands.

There are twelve baskets of fragments left over. They symbolise the abundance of Christ's compassion. They also herald the arrival of the Messianic age with its abundance of saving grace. These matters challenge the smallness of our own compassion.

Jesus, through today's gospel, signals and blesses the dual nature of our religion. He spends the whole day feeding the people's spirits with the good news of the kingdom of God and, 'as the day began to wear away,' he feeds their bodies with bread and fish.

We may take these lessons away with us from today's gospel. First, we are called to be very understanding of and compassionate with people. Second, our compassion must be practical and social. Third, our compassion should abound even as the multiplied bread and fish abounded and filled twelve extra baskets. Fourth, religion is about helping the whole person. The good news of God is social as well as spiritual in its meaning and in the range of its services.

And so, our worship of God here in this church, at this Mass, cannot be separated from social concern, and our liturgy cannot be divorced from life. That is why at the end of this Mass you will hear me say to you what you hear me say Sunday after Sunday: 'The Mass is ended. Let us go in peace to love and to serve the Lord and one another.'

Lessons from Cana

When the wine gave out, the mother of Jesus said to him, 'They have no wine.' ... Now six stone jars were standing there, for the Jewish rites of purification, each holding twenty or thirty gallons. Jesus said to the servants, 'Fill the jars with water.' And they filled them up to the brim. He said to them, 'Now draw some out, and take it to the steward of the feast.' So they took it. When the steward of the feast tasted the water now become wine ... he called the bridegroom and said to him, 'Every man serves the good wine first; and when men have drunk freely, then the poor wine; but you have kept the good wine until now.'

We can look at this scene of the wedding feast of Cana in three ways. Each has something to teach us.

Firstly, the story of the wedding feast of Cana is a human story. It has a down-to-earth touch about it. It involves a very human predicament. Jesus works his first public miracle in favour of a young bride and groom. His understanding and his humanity rescue the young couple from humiliation on their great day.

Some people may feel that the Lord could have chosen a more dramatic occasion for his first public miracle, and that he could have chosen more 'significant' people as its beneficiaries. But he didn't. He chose what he chose, and his choice turned out to be a young couple on their wedding day. Young people, married couples and families in general should note how important they must be in the priorities of Christ's heart.

Secondly, we find support in this gospel story for the Catholic tradition of going to God through his Blessed Mother, of bringing our needs to Jesus through Mary. Her influence with her Son is shown at Cana. She persuades Jesus to work his first miracle ahead of what may be called the time frame, or the proposed schedule, for his ministry. It is that time frame he is referring to when he says, 'My hour has not yet come.' It may be said, then, that Mary brings forward the hour of Christ's ministry, that she persuades him to work its first miracle before its time, so to speak, and to do so in favour of very ordinary people like ourselves. Now that she is in heaven in glory, is she not all the more empowered to persuade him to look with loving kindness on our needs?

Thirdly, we ask the meaning of this miracle in terms of the person of Jesus himself. For in this question's answer lies the main lesson of the story of Cana. John, our gospel writer, does not call Jesus' miracle a miracle but a sign. He says, 'This was the first of his signs, and by it he manifested his glory.' John means that the miracle of the water changed into wine is the first public sign of Jesus' Messiahship. This miracle, and the subsequent miracles of Jesus, are signs of the presence of the Messianic age and signs of Our Lord's true nature as the only Son of God.

In Hebrew numerology, six is an imperfect, an incomplete, number since seven is a complete or perfect number. Six stone jars are mentioned in the Cana story. They symbolise imperfection, incompleteness, deficiency. They represent, says William Barclay, 'all the imperfections of the law.' With the arrival of the Messiah the imperfections of the law become history, and Jesus puts in their tepid place 'the new wine of the gospel of his grace'.

There is no way that the religiously orthodox wedding guests at Cana would have been able to consume the contents of the six stone jars. Each held twenty-to-thirty gallons of wine! The immense amount of wine converted from water may be taken, then, to symbolise the abundance, and the overabundance, of God's grace now available to us under the Christian dispensation. We are being told that there is abundant grace for all of our legitimate needs. We are being told that there is life, and an abundance of it, for all who follow Christ and who are in Christ. We should not be surprised. For Jesus says later, in Jn 10:10, 'I am come that they may have life, and have it to the full.'

Actions, Not Words!

[Jesus] opened the book and found the place where it was written, 'The Spirit of the Lord is upon me, because he has anointed me to preach good news to the poor. He has sent me to proclaim release to the captives and recovery of sight to the blind, to set at liberty those who are oppressed, to proclaim the acceptable year of the Lord.' And he closed the book, and gave it back to the attendant, and sat down; and the eyes of all in the synagogue were fixed on him. And he began to say to them, 'Today this scripture has been fulfilled in your hearing.'

Actions speak louder than words. That's a saying we have all heard, but do not always follow. There are, indeed, times when we are all words and no action at all.

Margaret Thatcher is supposed to have said that if you want a speech written you should ask a man, but if you want something done you should ask a woman. Whatever the truth of that, the English essayist and statesman Francis Bacon cautioned that life is not for talk but for action. It is for living and doing and not just for looking at. In *The Advancement of Learning* he wrote, 'In the theatre of man's life it is reserved only for God and angels to be lookers-on.'

In today's gospel we find Jesus in the synagogue reading a section from the book of Isaiah. Isaiah is the Old Testament prophet who profiled, in advance, the promised Messiah. The Messiah would be identifiable not so much by what he would say as by what he would do. The core of the profile has the Messiah bringing the gospel of salvation to the poor, freeing people from their spiritual and physical bondages, and proclaiming a period of 'amnesty' or forgiveness from God. It is this core of the profile that Jesus selects when he stands up in the synagogue today and reads. When he finishes he says, 'Today this scripture is fulfilled.' What does he mean? He means that he is the Messiah profiled by Isaiah. And now the time has come for him to put the profile into action!

The reaction of the congregation to Jesus is that they 'fix their eyes' intently on him. They fix their eyes on him not because they are angry at him, but because they are riveted. They realise full well that he has just made the claim of Messiahship. And he does not sit down because he is finished but because – after the fashion of the rabbis – he is about to expound at length on the claim that he has just made.

I'm sure you remember the poignant scene in the gospel where John the Baptist is in prison awaiting death at the hands of King Herod. John had introduced Jesus to the people as the Messiah, and now he is having second thoughts about him. In his prison cell he wonders if Jesus really is the Messiah after all or has he, John, been deceived by a false Messiah. He had sent his disciples and the people flocking to Jesus when he said, 'Look, there is the Lamb of God. There is the Messiah. Follow him!' So now John sends messengers to Jesus with the question, 'Are you the One who is to come (i.e. the Messiah), or shall we look for another?' (Mt 11:3)

Jesus sends the messengers back with the proof of his Messiahship – he is doing precisely what Isaiah had profiled of the Messiah and his work: 'The blind receive their sight and the lame walk, lepers are cleansed and the deaf hear, and the dead are raised up, and the poor have the good news preached to them.' (Mt 11:4-5) Barclay observes of this exchange between Jesus and John the Baptist on Messiahship that Our Lord himself 'demanded that there should be applied to him the most acid of tests, that of deeds'.

The acid test of deeds over words never changes. Actions do speak louder than words. Jesus was a doer. His actions matched his words, or to put it another way, his words always materialised as actions. He said, 'My meat it is to do the will of him that sent me.' (Jn 4:34) Mary was a doer of God's word too. She said, 'I am the servant of the Lord. Let it be done to me as you say.' (Lk 1:38) Every saint is saint in the final analysis because he or she is a doer of the word and not just a hearer and an admirer of it. So, dear friends, let the challenge of the apostle James to the first Christians be the challenge to us as the latest Christians, 'Be doers of the word. If all you do is listen to it, you are deceiving yourselves.' (Jas 1: 22)

Us and Them

Jesus said, 'Truly, I say to you, no prophet is acceptable in his own country. But in truth, I tell you, there were many widows in Israel in the days of Elijah, when the heaven was shut up three years and six months, when there came a great famine over the land; and Elijah was sent to none of them but only to Zarephath, in the land of Sidon, to a woman who was a widow. And there were many lepers in Israel in the time of the prophet Elisha; and none of them was cleansed, but only Naaman the Syrian.' When they heard this, all in the synagogue were filled with wrath. And they rose up and put him out of the city, and led him to the brow of the hill on which their city was built, that they might throw him down headlong. But passing through the midst of them he went away.

Today's gospel is the continuation of the scene in the Nazareth synagogue which we heard about in last Sunday's gospel. You will remember that Jesus read a passage from the prophet Isaiah which referred to the Messiah to come, and when he had finished it he said, 'Today this scripture is fulfilled even as you listen.' He meant that he himself was the promised Messiah.

Those who listened to him were, at first, delighted with this good news. They 'fixed their eyes' intently on him, and 'they were amazed at the words of grace that came from his mouth.' (v 22) In today's gospel, however, there is a dramatic change of mood. They begin to have second thoughts about him. They say, 'Is not this Joseph's son?' And they have a grudge against him: he has not worked the spectacular miracles among them, here in his home town of Nazareth, that he has worked in Capernaum. And the grudge develops into hatred when he explains this supposed slighting of his home town and of themselves by telling them that 'a prophet is not acceptable in his own country.'

Then his listeners become infuriated when he seems to compliment the Gentiles, i.e. the non-Jewish pagan people. His orthodox listeners believe that the Gentiles know nothing of God, that they are merely 'fuel for the fires of hell'. But Jesus tells them that the greatest of the Jewish prophets, Elijah, was sent by God during a great famine not to comfort a Jewish widow but to comfort a Gentile widow. And he reminds them that the prophet Elisha cleansed the Gentile leper Naaman when he could have cleansed one or another of the many Jewish lepers of his day. Since Our Lord's listeners believed that they alone were God's people and that the hated Gentiles were outcasts, Jesus seemed to be showing a preference for the Gentiles and, thereby, insulting his orthodox Jewish listeners.

More truly, Our Lord is teaching them that his gospel of the good news from God is a socially inclusive gospel. It is the gospel for all peoples and all cultures and all times. It is a gospel of the wideness of the heart of God in contrast to the narrowness of their own Jewish heart. Rudyard Kipling wrote of English insularity in his time, 'All the people like us are We,/ And everyone else is They.' (*We and They*) The Jews of Our Lord's time followed this view of 'us and them' with regard to themselves and the hated Gentiles.

Are we afflicted with the 'us and them' mentality? Are we afflicted with it in terms of ourselves and immigrants, migrant workers, foreign students, single parents, gay children, and even upstanding fellow-citizens who just happen to live in the poorer part of town? And will we ever stop this social and unChristian snobbery?

I remember reading an American story years ago about a righteous old white Southern granny who, as the years brought the grave closer, was less and less sure whether heaven was all that worth getting into. It depended, she concluded finally, on whether you got to be with your 'own' or found yourself lumped in with 't'others.'

'T'others' were the Jews, the Mexicans, the Catholics and, above all, the Afro-Americans.

You and I, dear people, are followers of Christ. He holds us to his standards. We can have no part of the us-and-them mentality. How Jesus must have despised it, and how he almost paid the ultimate price in opposing it, as we see in today's gospel! 'They rose up and put him out of the city, and led him to the brow of the hill on which their city was built, that they might throw him down headlong. But passing through the midst of them he slipped away.'

Very Ordinary Men

When he had finished speaking, Jesus said to Simon, 'Put out into the deep and let down your nets for a catch.' And Simon answered, 'Master, we toiled all night and took nothing! But at your word I will let down the nets.' And when they had done this, they enclosed a great shoal of fish; and as their nets were breaking, they beckoned to their partners in the other boat to come and help them. And they came and filled both the boats, so that they began to sink. But when Simon Peter saw it, he fell down at Jesus' knees, saying, 'Depart from me, for I am a sinful man, O Lord.' ... And Jesus said to Simon, 'Do not be afraid; henceforth you will be catching men.' And when they brought their boats to land, they left everything and followed him.

In the old church biographies some of the saints were said to be 'born of noble parents' while others were said to be 'of humble origin'. Some came from the Big House and the big estate while others came from the labourers' cottages and the plots of the peasants. I've never known why the official church chose to make this distinction among the saints unless it be to show that sanctity can grow on either side of the fence.

In today's gospel, Jesus chooses four men as disciples. Later, these same four will be chosen as the first four apostles. None of them is born of noble parents and none is from the Big House. None has status, none is socially regarded, none is financially well-off (though the scholar Raymond Brown suggests they might be). They are four very ordinary men and, for Galileans, their trade could not be more ordinary. They are fishermen.

Did Jesus choose these ordinary men rather than more gifted and better-bred men because he was class conscious? No. I assume he chose them for their personal qualities and their potential, and because their immediate social circumstances allowed them, all the more easily, to hear his call and to respond to it. For they were not men encumbered with wealth and titles, or prejudiced by political office and party ties. They were not already biased in belonging to a particular rabbinical school of theology, nor had they to live up to great family expectations. They were simply fishermen whose lives seemed destined to be bookended by fish. In that sense they were available, and Jesus knew it. Unencumbered, they were able to respond to his call freely and immediately. That is why the gospel tells us that as soon as they brought their boats to land, 'they left everything and followed him.'

These very ordinary men had little to support their new and great destiny. They had only their fishing trade, confined to one lake all of their lives, and they had whatever religious formation they received at home and in their local synagogue. In this way, they carried no theological bias or social baggage that might obscure Christ's gospel and grace, and were therefore well-suited as novices for the Lord's fashioning. They were clean slates on which he could write his message of the good news from God.

To say that they were simple men is not a criticism but a compliment. Simple people are usually honest people. The four simple men Jesus called had big hearts and willing spirits, and maybe these were their most appealing attributes. They were exhausted from spending the whole night out on the lake catching nothing. Using the short 'casting' net, as the gospel implies, they would have cast their nets hundreds of times during the course of the night. Yet, at the Lord's word, they have the heart and the spirit to try again.

And when he called them there was no hesitation on their part. It may be that they could not but say yes to the attraction of this charismatic Christ. Most gospel commentators suggest the magnetism of the Lord's personality on them. On the other hand, perhaps they had seen and heard Jesus before by the lakeside, or in the streets of their lakeside village, and had long since been taken by his person and his teaching. Should he but offer them the invitation to follow him, they were predisposed to accept it. In today's gospel incident the invitation is offered, and that is why it is immediately and wholeheartedly accepted.

You and I also follow Jesus. We, too, are ordinary men and women by the standards of the world. We received his call at our baptism. Let us not allow empty sophistication and our good jobs and our new wealth, or bias or family expectations or social pressure, to get in the way of the Christian vocation that we have received. We ask the Lord for simplicity in our Christian lives, for the spirit of the gospel in our thoughts, and for a big heart in all that he calls us to do in his name.

A New Set of Values

Jesus lifted up his eyes over his disciples, and said, 'Blessed are you poor, for yours is the kingdom of God. Blessed are you that hunger now, for you shall be satisfied. Blessed are you that weep now, for you shall laugh. Blessed are you when men hate you, and when they revile you, and cast out your name as evil, on account of the Son of Man! Rejoice in that day, and leap for joy, for behold, your reward is great in heaven; for so their fathers did to the prophets. But woe to you that are rich, for you have received your consolation. Woe to you that are full now, for you shall hunger. Woe to you that laugh now, you shall mourn and weep. Woe to you when all men speak well of you, for so their fathers did to the false prophets'

Beatitudes are the subject of Our Lord in today's gospel. Jesus was not the originator of beatitudes. Beatitudes are blessings, and we find them scattered throughout the Old Testament long before Our Lord's time. However, when Christians say 'the beatitudes' they are referring to a specific group of eight blessings which Jesus announced in his sermon on the mount.

The beatitudes of Jesus reflect certain values. They are revolutionary values. They contradict the accepted values of the world of his time (and of ours too). Four of these beatitudes are named in today's gospel. In naming these four Jesus contrasts the happy state of the disciples who follow them with the sad condition of those who follow the values of the world.

Our Lord notes the limitations of the world's values. He points to what he calls the woeful state of the person who lives by them. Woe to the rich, he says, for they have already received all the consolation they are going to get. They have no future beyond this world. On the other hand, blessed are the disciples whose poverty exposes them to adversity. They withstand it because they have the gift of inner peace. And they are 'righteous'. They stand right with God now and will have a glorious future with him. Blessed are these poor who have nothing of the world's power and riches, but who rightly rely on God's providence instead.

Blessed are the disciples who hunger for righteousness before God and for justice for everyone, everywhere, and all the time. Blessed are the disciples who suffer loss and rejection and endure pain in forging their new Christian hearts. Blessed are the disciples who are reviled by the world for standing with Jesus, his gospel, and his values. Blessed are these possessors of a higher vision and of higher personal and social values.

But woe to the worldly for their narrow-visioned, narrow-hearted worldliness. Woe to them whose god is money and possessions and things. Woe to them because money and possessions and things are the limit of the comfort they now have or will ever get. Woe to those whose god is their belly: a famine of the spirit is their future. Woe to those who laugh and make merry in their worldliness: grief is the future of their empty souls. Woe to those who cut a dash with their popular theologies and hollow pieties, and who teach a religion that is worthless: their only destiny is the destiny of the false prophet and the false shepherd.

What are we to make of all of this? What is Jesus teaching us through these four beatitudes and their condemned opposites? Barclay's summation is plausible and worthwhile. He writes, 'If you set your heart and bend your whole energies to obtain the things which the world values, you will get them – but that is all you will ever get. If, on the other hand, you set your heart and bend all your energies to be utterly loyal to God and true to Christ, you will run into all kinds of trouble; you may by the world's standards look unhappy, but much of your payment is still to come; and it will be joy eternal.'

The Lord's Golden Rule

Jesus said, 'As you wish that men would do to you, do so to them.
Judge not, and you will not be judged; condemn not, and you will
not be condemned; forgive, and you will be forgiven; give, and it
will be given to you; good measure, pressed down, shaken together,
running over, will be put into your lap. For the measure you give
will be the measure you get back.'

The Golden Rule of Jesus is the line in today's gospel, 'As you
wish that people would do to you, so do to them.' It's another
way of saying treat people as you yourself wish to be treated. It
is such a simple rule, and it is at the heart of religion.

The Golden Rule is also found in Buddhist and in Islamic
writings. And it is found in the Old Testament, as we might expect, but usually in negative forms such as 'Do not do to anyone
what you yourself dislike.' (Tob 4:15) In Christian terms, it is
Our Lord's way of saying that we ought to love our neighbour
even to the degree that we love ourselves.

Just about everyone in the world has heard of the Golden
Rule in one form or another. And people who are not formally
religious find the rule written in their hearts and urging them, at
least in their better moments, to treat others as well as they
themselves like to be treated.

Despite this inborn or instinctive nature of the rule it is often
ignored. Most of the sad stories we read in the papers or see
fleshed-out on television are the consequences of ignoring the
Golden Rule. War, terrorism, abuse, violence, greed, jealousy
and neglect result from the lack of love in the human family.
Even the church, past and present, cannot escape the charge of
ignoring the Golden Rule. The novelist Morris West writes of
the contemporary church, 'Love has been lost to us.' (*A View
From The Ridge*) He writes from personal experience with church
authorities as well as from awareness of present-day abuses
within the church. Love has been lost, he writes, on the leadership level through the misuse of authority. He and you and I
have seen this misuse most recently in the saga of child abuse
and episcopal cover-up.

And what of secular society? Does it stand the test of the

Golden Rule? We have our tribunals and inquiries and commissions whose very existence, whatever their conclusions, sign our society's contradictions of the Golden Rule. Citizens, too, are the victims of others' crooked schemes and scams. We have Consumer Affairs reports on over-pricing in goods and under-performance in services. Locks and alarm systems are commonplace because assault and burglary are now as frequent as head colds in winter. Our society is not exactly dripping with the love of the neighbour at the moment, and whole chunks of it are very far removed from the Golden Rule.

Some of us feel that it's asking too much to live by the Golden Rule anymore. For one thing, our twenty-first century neighbours are simply not what neighbours used to be, and it's very hard to love them. They're forever groaning and griping. They're outraged at everything and gutted at nothing, and they wouldn't hesitate about taking you to court if there's a bit of money to be got there.

For all of that, the Golden Rule remains, and it continues to confront and to challenge us. It is at the heart of religion, and of social sanity. It challenges us to keep pushing ourselves outward in love of others and to keep pulling these others inward to our hearts, and all the more so in this age of suspicion and anonymity. Of course it involves the element of risk, but risk has always been of the nature of love. We know in our bones that the Golden Rule is right as religion and right as social ethic, and that our world would be paradise if we treated one another as each of us wishes to be treated. We all want to be treated with love, and we always will. Such is the practicality and the endurability of the Golden Rule.

When we are tempted to say, 'I'll treat them nice when they start treating me nice,' we will tell ourselves instead that this is only a variation of something Our Lord condemned, the *quid pro quo*, the eye for an eye and the tooth for a tooth. We have to move beyond the eye and the tooth stage in our relationships or we might end up with a neighbourhood full of the blind and the toothless.

The Golden Rule is the rule of love with the solutions of love. Barclay would have us look to God, rather than to neighbour, for inspiration to get beyond the self-concern and the suspicion, and embrace the Golden Rule. 'It is not our neighbour with whom we must compare ourselves; we may well stand that comparison adequately. It is God with whom we must compare ourselves.' God's selfless love for us is our motivation for loving others even though we know that our love of others will never quite match the depth and the breadth of God's proven love of us.

Additional Rules for Living

Jesus said, 'No good tree bears bad fruit, nor again does a bad tree bear good fruit; for each tree is known by its own fruit. Figs are not gathered from thorns, nor are grapes picked from a bramble bush. The good man out of the good treasure of his heart produces good, and the evil man out of his evil treasure produces evil; for out of the abundance of the heart his mouth speaks.'

In last Sunday's gospel Our Lord gave us the Golden Rule. In today's gospel he gives us additional rules for Christian living. Luke may have gathered here these rules or sayings of Jesus from one or more unrelated contexts as the scholars suggest. At any rate, they fit comfortably enough as addenda to the Golden Rule.

In the last section of today's gospel Jesus stresses deeds over words, action in place of talk. He says that a good tree produces good fruit and a bad tree produces bad fruit. Let us take the good tree to mean the true disciple of Jesus. The bad tree is the false or nominal disciple. The true disciple produces Christlike deeds, and produces them in abundance.

A challenge to the churches today is the presence of so many nominal members. Nominal members are members who do not have what is called a living or a lived faith. They are not dynamically involved with faith or church. They are basically uncatechised and inactive members. They have been baptised, communioned and confirmed sure enough but there is little evidence of the effect of these sacraments in their lives. They are card-carrying but not committed Christians. None of this is said to excuse ourselves or to suggest that there is no room for Christian improvement in our own lives. There always is.

The German philosopher Nietzsche has greatly influenced our Western world, its religious decline, and what is called the secular mentality. He may have been the first to coin the phrase, 'God is dead.' How is God dead? For many Westerners, God is dead in the sense that science and technology offer them real solutions to their real problems and God, consequently, is 'surplus to requirement.' But for Nietzsche himself, God is dead because his followers – that's us – have not kept him alive! We do not sufficiently reflect his face, show his heart, or be his healing hands in the world. In fact, says Nietzsche, there has ever been only one Christian and that Jesus himself. There have been no other Christians, he argues, because none ever came close to being a copy of Christ. 'Only Christian practice, a life such as he who died on the Cross lived, is Christian.' (*The Antichrist*)

We ought not react woundedly and stop our ears to the challenge of Nietzsche's words, 'Only Christian practice, a life such as he who died on the Cross lived, is Christian.' It is a tough challenge surely, but it gets to the heart of being a Christian. It's the call to Christian action in place of Christian talk. It's the challenge to live the gospel.

Jesus offers the same challenge today. The good tree is not the tree that looks good: it is the tree that bears good fruit. Jesus says, 'The good man out of the good treasure of his heart produces good.' The abundant heart expresses itself in abundant deeds, not in abundant words. Dean Inge once said, 'Religion is a way of walking, not a way of talking.' (*Outspoken Essays*)

Jesus tells us that we only really teach by example. We can only lead others to where we have arrived ourselves. The Christian life is not about searching out the faults of others, but about attacking the greater faults in ourselves. We cannot see clearly enough to remove the mote from our brother's eye while a big beam remains stuck in our own. Our Christian life is about practice, not theory. It's about doing, not saying. It's a way of walking, not a way of talking. It is about the good deeds of faith, hope and love, and an abundance of them.

Faith and Tolerance

A centurion had a slave who was dear to him, who was sick and at the point of death. When he heard of Jesus, he sent to him elders of the Jews, asking him to come and heal his slave ... When Jesus was not far from the house, the centurion sent friends to him, saying to him, 'Lord, do not trouble yourself, for I am not worthy to have you come under my roof ... But say the word, and let my servant be healed. For I am a man set under authority, with soldiers under me: and I say to one, "Go," and he goes; and to another, "Come," and he comes; and to my slave, "Do this," and he does it.' When Jesus heard this he marvelled at him, and turned and said to the multitude that followed him, 'I tell you, not even in Israel have I found such faith.' And when those who had been sent returned to the house, they found the slave well.

It is said that no one is completely tolerant, and that everyone has large or small prejudices. This holds true also for religious people. Some of our critics say it holds true especially for religious people. In his last interview, in 1994 on Channel 4, the playwright Dennis Potter said to Melvyn Bragg, 'Religion to me has always been the wound, not the bandage.' Potter's view of religion may be extreme but I find it alive and well in the heads of some of my third-level students.

We agree with Potter that awful things have been done down the centuries in the name of God and religion by religious people. In our own time we've seen plenty of religious bigotry and brutality at home and abroad, courtesy of the television cameras. The classical writer Lucretius long ago noted 'the heights of wickedness to which men are driven by religion' (*On The Nature Of The Universe*) None of this should happen, of course, but it has and it still does.

You and I, quite naturally, like to believe that evil things are not done by religious people but by people pretending to be religious and by people using religion as a cover for their darkness. But the facts insist that we do not hide our heads in the sand. It is true that many non-religious leaders have faked religiosity or used religion to attain their evil purposes, but it is also true that many religious people have done and still do terrible things.

We've all seen the Yugoslav tanks coming out of Muslim Kosovo with their Orthodox Christian crews giving the TV cameras the sign of the Blessed Trinity – ethnic cleansing of Muslims in the name of the Christian God. And we've seen the hijacked aircraft smashed into the World Trade Center, those twin-towering symbols of 'the Great Satan,' and their innocent victims vaporised in the name of Allah. These atrocities are examples of religion as the wound and not the bandage.

What can be done about it? The leaders of the great religions, churches, mosques, and synagogues may not be able to do much about evil people who fake religiosity but there is much they can do about the religious education and formation of their own memberships. They must cleanse the hearts and educate the minds of those members who still believe that bigotry and hate and death have a place in religion. There are still too many believers in all the religions whose religious ignorance allows them to be the ready tools of evil and of those who style themselves 'the hammer of God.'

Today's gospel presents the type of religious person we ought to imitate. He is the centurion. The centurion teaches tolerance. He teaches the death of bigotry. The centurion is a Gentile, yet he is a man of deep faith. He is a man of concern for another's welfare. He is tolerant of other peoples' religions. His concern and his tolerance are eminently practical. He sends for Our Lord on behalf of the sick slave whose worth may be less, at that time in history, than the price of a donkey. And he has already done an astounding thing: he has built a synagogue for the Jews at a time when Jew and Gentile hate the dust of the ground the other walks upon.

True believers can not be prejudiced or bigoted or hateful people, nor merchants of death and destruction in the name of God. Religion continues to be, in part, the story of these awful things. It continues to be, in part, the wound instead of the bandage. Today we ask the Lord for the gift of the centurion's faith, a concerned faith, and for the active servant love he had. And we ask the Lord for a deeper commitment to our own beloved Christian faith even as we ask him to expand our tolerance of other peoples' cherished beliefs.

Christ's Compassion and Ours

As [Jesus] drew near the gate of the city, behold, a man who had died was being carried out, the only son of his mother, and she was a widow; and a large crowd from the city was with her. And when the Lord saw her, he had compassion on her and said to her, 'Do not weep.' And he came and touched the bier, and the bearers stood still. And he said, 'Young man, I say to you arise.' And the dead man sat up, and began to speak. And he gave him to his mother.

Life is boring for many people. The days come and go, and the years multiply, and they find themselves doing the same things over and over. They go through the same old routines and rituals, and repeat the same old trivialities. 'I have measured out my life with coffee spoons,' says Prufrock in T. S. Eliot's *Love Song of J. Alfred Prufrock.* Some of us, perhaps, measure it out with golf balls or glasses of the black stuff!

Other people have an acute sense of life's pain. They are offended by the suffering, the angst, and the pull and drag of life. Life has its moments, of course, but mostly it's a struggle. It wears them down. It can be grim. So much so that the poet, Robert Browning, called life 'that insane dream.' (*Easter-Day*)

Life drives others to depression. It almost drove the Christian philosopher, Soren Kierkegaard, to the wall. He wrote, 'Great is my sorrow, without limits. None knows of it, except God in heaven, and he cannot have pity.' (W. H. Auden, *A Kierkegaard Anthology*)

Today's gospel contradicts Kierkegaard. It portrays a God, through Christ, who has pity and who does something about the pain. In Christ, God is pity personified. We need to say something about the word 'pity' because it is a word that has fallen on bad times. Nobody wants to be pitied these days because it implies helplessness and lack of worth. People say, 'Don't pity me!' and 'I don't need your pity!' However, we need to remember that in the gospel pity is a beautiful word. It stands for the compassion of God.

Jesus comes upon a funeral. A young man is being carried out of the city for burial. His poor mother is distraught, for he is an only son and she is a widow. She has lost her only son and that means she has lost her security. Jesus is moved to pity. To be moved to pity means to suffer with someone at the level of their pain. Jesus is troubled in heart, touched at his core. It is not the death of the young man that wounds his heart so much as the plight of the widowed mother.

The great advantage of 'God being in Christ,' to use St Paul's expression, was that God was thus able to incarnate his compassion for people and the people were able to experience it in visible, tangible form. God became a hands-on God in Christ. He moved among his children with active compassion. Christ is gone now but God's compassion continues in sacramental forms, and in dramatic forms such as the cures at Lourdes, and in less dramatic forms such as we read about in the newspapers under 'Thanksgiving for Blessings Received,' and in that gentle form by which faith and grace lessen our pain and assure us of God's protective arms about us.

There is yet another incarnation of God's pity and compassion. It is an incarnation intended by God for this time of Our Lord's absence, the time between his ascension and his coming in glory. This particular incarnation of God's pity and compassion is in and through our very selves. Christ has called us to be the care and the loving kindness of God to our own time and place. Jesus left this world saying, 'As the Father sent me, even so I send you.' (Jn 20:21) Our sending by him includes our sending to be the pity and the compassion of God upon others in their trouble and pain. Therefore, let us ask for the gift that is necessary in order that we be God's compassion in our own time and place: the gift of a heart capable of being troubled and touched at its core by the plight of others, as the Lord's heart was so touched at the sight of the widow of Naim.

Driven by Love

One of the Pharisees asked Jesus to eat with him, and he went to the Pharisee's house, and took his place at table. And behold, a woman of the city, who was a sinner, when she learned that he was at table in the Pharisee's house, brought an alabaster flask of ointment, and standing behind him at his feet, weeping, she began to wet his feet with her tears, and wiped them with the hair of her head, and kissed his feet, and anointed them with the ointment. Now when the Pharisee who had invited him saw it, he said to himself, 'If this man were a prophet, he would have known who and what sort of woman this is who is touching him, for she is a sinner.' And Jesus answering said to him, 'Simon, I have something to say to you.' ... 'I entered your house, you gave me no water for my feet, but she has wet my feet with her tears and wiped them with her hair. You gave me no kiss, but from the time I came in she has not ceased to kiss my feet. You did not anoint my head with oil, but she has anointed my feet with ointment. Therefore I tell you, her sins, which are many, are forgiven, for she loved much; but he who is forgiven little, loves little.'

When John Wayne starts walking out Maureen O'Hara in *The Quiet Man* their first outing is on Barry Fitzgerald's side-car. He reminds them stiffly that there is to be no sitting side-by-side, and no hand-holding or stuff of that sort. Rather, says he, 'The proprieties are to be observed at all times.'

The Pharisee who invites Jesus to dinner forgets to observe the Jewish proprieties which he should have offered to his invited guest. He seems more intent on sizing-up Jesus and wondering why a man with a prophet's reputation doesn't know that a prostitute is sitting at his feet. The woman is actually doing her best to supply the proprieties which the Pharisee failed to offer Jesus. Jesus is well-aware of what the woman is doing and aware that the Pharisee, with his head held high in disdain, is not. So the Lord says to the Pharisee, 'Simon, I have something to say to you.' The Lord proceeds to tell Simon, item by item, how the woman has supplied all the proprieties of welcome. She has supplied them as best she could.

A Jewish guest was entitled to a formal *shalom* welcome, and to the kiss of greeting if he was a rabbi. Jesus was known as a rabbi. Simon gave no kiss of greeting, but the woman kissed the Lord's feet. A bowl of water should have been provided to wash the dust of the road from the guest's feet. Simon provided none, but the woman washed the Lord's feet with her tears. Simon provided no towel to dry the feet, so the woman used her hair. The guest's feet should have been perfumed after drying. Simon provided no perfumed oil, but the woman took her Jewish woman's phial of perfume from around her neck and poured it on the Lord's feet.

Perhaps the two most significant details in the whole incident are the woman's tears of sorrow for her sins and her manifest love of Jesus. In stark contrast are Simon's two omissions: his lack of the proprieties of welcome and his singular lack of love. Simon, like a lot of people in religion and out of it, really neither cares a lot nor loves a lot. Our Lord is just an object of theological interest or of public notoriety to him, and the prostitute is basically a non-person and a social and religious pollution in his house. But Jesus says, 'Her many sins are forgiven because of her great love.' She is at the heart of religion with her repentance and her love: Simon, the man of religion, is far from it.

Barclay makes the comment: 'The better a man is the more he feels his sin.' It is the good person who is most aware of his or her sin, and no one has a finer sense of sin than a saint. No one feels more a sinner than a saint. The saint always sees himself or herself as the greatest sinner in the world and the most abject of God's creatures. We can say of the prostitute in today's gospel that she was well along the road to sanctity, for she wept over her sins and was driven by her love to the Lord's forgiveness.

In response to this gospel, you and I might ask the Lord to forgive us our sins of omission: the things we should do but don't do, and the things we should have done but didn't do. And may he forgive our sins of inhospitality too: the hand not offered when it should have been, and the welcoming word not spoken. And we might ask Our Lord for the gift of tears, the gift that the woman in today's gospel had in abundance. It is a gift hardly mentioned at all by the spiritual writers of our generation, and yet it is the grace every true saint is gifted with. The gift of tears is the measure of our sorrow for sin and the measure of the depth of our love of God.

Christian Identity

Now it happened that as Jesus was praying alone the disciples were with him; and he asked them, 'Who do the people say that I am?' And they answered, 'John the Baptist; but others say, Elijah; and others, that one of the old prophets has risen.' And he said to them, 'But who do you say that I am?' And Peter answered, 'The Christ of God.' But he charged and commanded them to tell this to no one, saying, 'The Son of Man must suffer many things, and be rejected by the elders and chief priests and scribes, and be killed, and on the third day be raised.' And he said to all, 'If any man would come after me, let him deny himself and take up his cross daily and follow me. For whoever would save his life will lose it; and whoever loses his life for my sake, he will save it.'

When the Australian writer Morris West left the religious life he had a problem. He was still a young man. His parting from his religious congregation was cold. He looked back on his training as a novice as 'an exercise in bigotry'. His earlier religious and social background was narrow and reactionary. He called it a growing-up with 'unexamined conviction'. So he 'returned to the world' very ignorant of its language and its ways, and considerably lost. He set about 'trying to assemble the elements of my fragmented identity'. (*A View From The Ridge*)

Many people suffer an identity crisis. They don't know who they are. Most of them try to find out. They work at discovering themselves. Some don't, and suffer the consequences. None of us, of course, knows the depth of the inner self and what might happen there under certain circumstances. What we do know is that our self-identity is fragile and vulnerable. You and I, as believers, are more sure of our identity than many others. I do not say that in a condescending way. I say it in a purely grateful way. We are grateful to God for the gift of our faith because it shapes so much of our self-understanding and self-identity.

Primo Levi, a survivor of the infamous Auschwitz extermination camp, tells us what faith means in terms of one's identity and its sustaining value. Himself an agnostic, he writes of Auschwitz, 'In the grind of everyday life the believers lived better ... Catholic or Reformed priests, rabbis of the various orthodoxies, militant Zionists, naïve or sophisticated Marxists and Jehovah's Witnesses – all held in common the saving force of their faith. Their world was vaster than ours ... above all more comprehensible. They had a key and a point of leverage ... a place in heaven or on earth where justice and compassion had won, or would win in a perhaps remote but certain future.' (*The Drowned And The Saved*)

Our Christian faith is a great gift in terms of our self-understanding and self-identity. To use Levi's words, it is our saving force, our key to life's confusion and crosses and mystery, our spur in pursuing justice and in practising compassion. Being a Christian is very much at the core of our identity. In today's gospel, Our Lord defines some of the key elements of the Christian identity. Let us refresh our minds with them.

Jesus asks his disciples, 'Who do you say that I am?' Peter answers, 'You are the Christ of God, you are God's anointed One.' We answer Our Lord's question in the same confident manner. And we place all our trust in him.

Jesus specifically wanted to know what his own disciples thought of him. This introduces the personal nature of faith. We do not only state our faith as a set of beliefs but internalise and personalise it. Jesus is not only the Saviour and Lord of the world: he is my Saviour and my Lord. I accept him as such. And I try to imitate his life in my own. I take up my cross in imitation of his. My cross is the daily grind and the ups and downs of the day. And it is the denial of my own selfishness, and the putting of others and their concerns at the centre of my world. In these I find meaning and purpose. And much of my identity.

Once Again – Tolerance!

When the days drew near for him to be received up, he set his face to go to Jerusalem. And he sent messengers ahead of him, who went and entered a village of the Samaritans, to make ready for him; but the people would not receive him, because his face was set toward Jerusalem. And when his disciples James and John saw it, they said, 'Lord, do you want us to bid fire come down from heaven and consume them?' But he turned and rebuked them. And they went on to another village.

In her book, *Waiting On God*, Simone Weil writes of believers who 'have faith exclusively in [their own] religion and only bestow upon the others the sort of attention we give to strangely shaped shells.' Dean Swift wrote incisively of Christians having 'just enough religion to ... hate.' (*Thoughts On Various Subjects*) History puts flesh on these observations in the clash of denominations and religious cultures. We see them at work in our own time in Yugoslavia, the Sudan, East Timor, the Middle East, Northern Ireland and the smashing of the Twin Towers. These are illustrations of 'just enough religion to ... hate.'

The awful stuff that is done in the name of God, in the name of Allah, is blasphemy. Let us not fudge here as religious leaders do. There is no other word for it. 'Have we not all one Father? Did not the one God create us?' (Mal 2:10) The God we all worship is one and the same God that the angels adore when they bow down in worship and say, 'Holy, holy, holy is the Lord of Hosts.' (Is 6:3)

Why do some people, then, hate and hate viciously in the name of God who is the Father of all? Is it because religion is only a veneer in the lives of many? Is it because some people are psychologically incapable of grasping the message of love which is at the heart of all religion? Or is it a matter of chronic religious ignorance, and thus of the failure – or the absence – of religious education? Or is it due to the continuing failure of the various world religious leaderships to prevent the politicisation of their religious systems?

In today's gospel Jesus 'sets his face' for Jerusalem. It will be his last journey to the holy city, because he is going to suffer and to die there. He sends messengers ahead to prepare a village to receive him. The village is on the road to Jerusalem. It is a Samaritan village. The Samaritans are people who are despised by the Jews. The two groups hate each other for religious reasons. But Jesus wants to share the gospel of salvation with the Samaritans even as he shares it with the orthodox Jews. What happens? They refuse to welcome him to their village. Why? Because he is going up to Jerusalem, the holy city of the hated Jews.

To make matters worse, his disciples James and John are enraged by the refusal of these Samaritans. 'Lord, would you like us to call down fire from heaven to consume them?' Would Our Lord like to see the Samaritans incinerated – in the name of God? How far removed are not even these chosen disciples from understanding God as love, their Lord as the world's Saviour, and his gospel as a message of saving love! Which circumstance disturbed Our Lord more: the religious hate of the Samaritans or the violent reaction of his Christian apostles? Both must have afflicted Our Lord's heart at this late stage of his teaching and ministry. His three years in their company appear to have taught them nothing at all. We may apply Swift's words to these apostles – just enough religion to hate, but not enough to love.

And what of you and me? What of the quality of the religion we practise? We know that people divide themselves by nationality and community, into exclusive groups and camps, and by religion as well. In the process, they tend to create insiders and outsiders, those who belong and those who don't. When this is carried too far we end up with sinful discrimination and exclusion. There are Christians, as you and I well know, who have little love for one another because of some unfortunate business or legal incident in the past, or because of a failed marriage, or because of expectations not met. You know as I do how we sometimes expect others to live their lives according to the scripts we write for them rather than by the scripts only they have the right to write for themselves. You know as I do that trust betrayed and old hurts, like old soldiers, never die and that their unintended remembrance can surprise with the blush of anger or the rush of hate.

If these are the kinds of things which undermine the quality of our religion, we must do our best to let go of them. They harm us more than they could possibly harm those who are the object of our anger and hate. We need to turn them over to the Lord, and ask him to take ownership of them in our place. He brought them all to the cross a long time ago, and it's about time we left them there. If we hold on to them, they will simmer on the back-burner of our hearts and they will tempt us, every now and then, to call down fire and destruction on others as the irate apostles wished to call it down on the Samaritans. Our behaviour, then, will be as disappointing to the Lord as theirs was to him in today's gospel story.

14th Sunday of the Year: Gospel: Lk 10: 1-12, 17-20

Building the Kingdom

After this the Lord appointed seventy-two others, and sent them on ahead of him, two by two, into every town and place where he himself was about to come. And he said to them, 'The harvest is plentiful, but the labourers are few; pray therefore the Lord of the harvest to send out labourers into his harvest. Go your way ... and say to them, "The kingdom of God has come near to you".'

Stephen Foster puts these words on the lips of Old Black Joe in his plantation song of that name: 'No more rain fall for wet you, hallelujah./No more sun shine for burn you./There's no hard trials,/There's no whips a-cracking,/No evildoers in the kingdom,/All is gladness in the kingdom, hallelujah!'

Afro-American slaves like Old Black Joe experienced life as a burden, and death was a blessed release. The kingdom of God of which Old Black Joe sang was not the kingdom of God on earth but the kingdom of God in heaven. Old Black Joe would not have understood our theology which makes the kingdom of God a kingdom of love and peace and justice here on earth, and even in the slave fields where cotton was king.

Neither, for that matter, would the *spailpíní* of my childhood have understood God's kingdom as a plan for this earth, nor would the English industrial workers of the time of Old Black Joe. 'Their lot was as bad as anything which could be told of the plantations,' writes Hugh Brogan in *The Penguin History of the USA*.

In today's gospel Jesus sends out seventy-two disciples, additional to the twelve apostles already sent, to preach the kingdom of God and to help lay its foundations. So, what is the kingdom? And where is it? The kingdom is the rule of God over our hearts now and the rule love and peace and justice in all we do. It is the restructuring of ourselves and of our society so that we live by love and peace and justice. It is the building of a better earth. Its values are opposed to the grasping values of the unredeemed world. We know that unredeemed world all too well, as did Old Black Joe and the *spailpíní* and the English industrial workers. It is still around. We live in it, suffer from it, and see its sins fleshed out in the daily TV news stories.

The kingdom of God is the unredeemed world's adversary. The kingdom of God is its replacement. The kingdom of God is the new plan for this world. The kingdom is now and it is concrete. 'There is no reason for thinking,' writes theologian Albert Nolan, 'that the kingdom floats in the air somewhere above the earth or that it is an abstract entity without any tangible social and political structure.' (*Jesus Before Christianity*) If we want to see the kingdom detailed as the new plan for this earth, we can do no better than read the social encyclicals of the popes from Leo XIII to John Paul II.

The kingdom is for the here and now. It is future in the sense that it is always a task before us, and that it is always capable of qualitative increase. When we pray, 'Thy kingdom come,' we are praying that God's just and loving will be done as perfectly on this earth as it is already done perfectly in heaven by the angels. We pray, 'Thy kingdom come,' because there is always room for the kingdom's more intense presence in our hearts and in the world.

The gospel of the Lord is not only a programme by which we may attain heaven but also a plan for living life on this earth. When very many people live the rule of the kingdom of God their combined goodness necessarily impacts our society and our world for the better. The widespread practise of the Christian life builds the better society and the better earth for, as Leonardo Boff notes, kingdom people are not isolated islands 'but a continent ... involved with and impacting others.' (*Liberating Grace*)

For Old Black Joe the kingdom of God was never something for this world. It could only be a dream for the next. We cannot fault him as an illiterate slave in the holding pens called cotton fields. Let us pray, then, for the grace of being kingdom-committed people, people of that teaching which was central to Christ's message, and the theology closest to his heart. Let us pray for deeper insight into God's will for us. We ask for the gift of greater commitment to living our lives by Christ's measures. We seek ever more just and generous hearts. Only such will allow us to fashion the kingdom of love and justice and peace in our own place and time, and only such will manifest to others the kingdom of God at work in their midst.

Who is my Neighbour?

And behold, a lawyer stood up to put him to the test, saying,
'Teacher, what shall I do to inherit eternal life?' [Jesus] said to him,
'What is written in the law? How do you read?' And he answered,
'You shall love the Lord your God with all your heart, and with all
your soul, and with all your strength, and with all your mind; and
your neighbour as yourself.' And he said to him, 'You have an-
swered right; do this, and you will live.' But he, desiring to justify
himself, said to Jesus, 'And who is my neighbour?'

Jewish people in Our Lord's time, as Christian people in our
time, knew that love of neighbour was a requirement of the law
of God. They even knew, as we know, that the neighbour is to be
loved as deeply and as widely as one loves oneself. The unclear
issue was, who exactly is my neighbour?

The rabbis and the lawyers normally defined the neighbour
as fellow-Jews. They detested the Gentiles and despised the
Samaritans so that these groups, among others, were not neighbours to be loved. The lawyer in today's gospel asks Our Lord a
very honest question. He wants to know who precisely is the
neighbour that is to be loved. Is it only one's fellow-Jew? Jesus
answers him with the story of the Good Samaritan.

The Samaritans were regarded as heretics. They were the descendants of Jews who had been exiled to northern Israel, to the
province called Samaria, by the Assyrians about 700 years before Christ. They accepted only the 'Samaritan Pentateuch,' the
first five books of the Bible, as the word of God and they looked
on their own Mt Gerizim rather than Mt Zion (Jerusalem) as
God's sanctuary. Living in the borderlands of Israel, they had in-
termarried with neighbouring Gentiles. This made them all the
more abominable to Jerusalem and to orthodox Judaism.

Our Lord's story tells of a man travelling on the road between Jerusalem and Jericho. It was a road of twists and turns. It
was ideal for ambush and, hence, for robbers. It was known as
the red road, or the road of blood, because of the frequency of
the attacks on travellers. It is no surprise then that the travelling
man in Our Lord's story is attacked by robbers. They beat him
up, rob him, and leave him half-dead. Along comes a priest. He

is Jewish, religious, orthodox. He looks at the unfortunate man but quickly passes by 'on the other side' of the road. Along comes a Levite, also Jewish, religious, and orthodox. He too quickly passes by 'on the other side.'

Then comes a Samaritan, a man regarded by the other two as half-pagan, defiled, unorthodox. He stops, binds up the poor man's wounds, takes him to the nearest inn, and arranges for his care. In so doing he risks being attacked himself. In addition, he undertakes to check on the wounded man on his return journey and to take care of any additional costs. Our Lord asks the lawyer to name which one of the three was neighbour to the stricken man. The lawyer answers, 'He who showed mercy.' Our Lord says, 'Go, and do likewise.'

Neither the lawyer nor we know anything of the stricken man. We know nothing about his nationality, religion or social circumstances. We are not meant to. We are being taught that love of neighbour is blind to any and all such matters. Love's only consideration is the need of a fellow-human being. Our neighbour, then, is any human being in need. And who in our world isn't in need in one way or another?

For most of us, the neighbour is the person we know, and the person next door, and the few families on either side of our house. We feel we cannot risk extending the definition to include the entire neighbourhood because there are, regrettably, good and bad patches in all neighbourhoods, and these are anonymous and suspicious days. We feel that it is pushing the envelope of prudence were we to include under neighbour people we don't really know, and 'all these new people in our country' who differ from us in race, colour, culture and religion. But this is the envelope Jesus pushed with his story of the Good Samaritan and the anonymous victim. The Christian envelope is an all-inclusive one when it comes to another human being in need.

The neighbour, then, is any child of God in need. Or as William Barclay puts it, 'Any man of any nation who is in need is our neighbour. Our help must be as wide as the love of God.'

The Good Portion

Now as they went on their way, [Jesus] entered a village; and a woman named Martha received him into her house. And she had a sister called Mary, who sat at the Lord's feet and listened to his teaching. But Martha was distracted with much serving; and she went to him and said, 'Lord, do you not care that my sister has left me to serve alone? Tell her then to help me.' But the Lord answered her, 'Martha, Martha, you are anxious and troubled about many things; one thing is needful. Mary has chosen the good portion, which shall not be taken from her.'

Martha and Mary were two sisters. Their brother was Lazarus. They lived in Bethany near Jerusalem. It would seem that Our Lord knew them well and had stayed in their home on his way to and from the holy city. Most scholars believe that Lazarus was a disciple of Jesus.

One of these visits of Our Lord is the subject of today's gospel. Martha is the more forward of the two sisters. But we should read that positively. She is the active and the practical one. The late Archbishop Jules Saliège of Toulouse described her as 'always lively and on the move.' (*Spiritual Writings*) She is concerned with Jewish hospitality and conscious of its requirements in Our Lord's regard.

Nevertheless, our gospel drops the hint that Martha crossed over the line which separates the legitimate concerns of hospitality from fussiness when it notes that she was 'distracted with much serving.' All the commentators say that a simple meal would be sufficient to fulfil the law of hospitality on an informal occasion such as this one was, but Martha was having none of it. All her fussing and fretting seems to have given her a short fuse too. She interrupts Our Lord as he speaks with Mary, who is listening intently to him. Martha seems to scold both of them when she says, 'Lord, do you not care that my sister has left me to serve alone? Tell her then to help me.' You get the impression that Martha is not only absorbed in her work but insists that Mary should be absorbed in it too. She appears to be a somewhat controlling person and we might not be blamed if we saw her, partly, as the model for Frank Sinatra's signature song, *I Did It My Way*.

You know the Lord's reply. He tells Martha that she is anxious and troubled about many things but not concerned about the one thing necessary, 'the good portion'. On the other hand, 'the good portion' is Mary's only and consuming concern. And Our Lord says that it shall not be taken from her. What is 'the good portion'? The NAB translation reads, 'the better portion.' Tradition has used the two women to represent the active and the contemplative aspects of the church: its missionaries in the field and the enclosed religious whose prayers and contemplation support them. Tradition has also seen, in the contrast of Martha and Mary, the Lord's selection of the contemplative life over the active life. These understandings of the incident in Bethany seem to stretch its interpretation.

The Lord is on his way to the holy city. He will not be returning to Bethany. The hour of his passion and death is at hand. His spirit must be absorbed now with foreboding and with what Barclay calls 'the intensity of the inner battle to bend his will to the will of God'. And here is Martha absorbed to the point of distraction with the details of hospitality and with preparing a big meal! Neither of these things is meaningful to Jesus at this moment. Martha is so busy she does not seem to notice Our Lord's anxious condition. But Mary does. She sits at Our Lord's feet listening to him. The gospel says she is listening 'to his words.' (NAB) The words may be holy words, or they may be the anxious words of a man on his way to die. Mary listens with what we may presume is sensitive understanding and compassionate love. This is the better portion, and Mary has chosen it. It is the form of hospitality and the kind of attention Jesus needs in this hour.

Romano Guardini once said that Jesus, in obedience to his Father's will, came unto his own but his distracted own did not receive him. 'He spoke the word ... but his message found deaf ears ... He summoned humankind to share in divine life ... but humankind declined, and the Messenger of love was left standing in immeasurable isolation.' (*The Lord*) Mary is a great exception to our human insensitivity. She chooses the good portion. She is our model for listening to the word of God, even for being absorbed in it, and for listening to the pain of Christ in the pain of others and responding with all the attentive love our hearts can summon.

The Lord's Prayer

[Jesus] was praying in a certain place, and when he ceased, one of his disciples said to him, 'Lord, teach us to pray, as John taught his disciples.' And he said to them, 'When you pray, say, "Father, hallowed be thy name. Thy kingdom come. Give us each day our daily bread; and forgive us our sins, for we ourselves forgive every one who is indebted to us; and lead us not into temptation".'

It was customary for every important rabbi or holy man to teach his followers a unique prayer. This would normally be a summary prayer, or a formula prayer, based on his teaching and easy to remember. Some of Our Lord's disciples had previously been John the Baptist's disciples, and one of them asks Jesus to teach them a unique prayer. Jesus responds with what we call the Lord's Prayer or the Our Father.

In Matthew's gospel the Our Father is given during the Sermon on the Mount – during the central teaching of Jesus – and, as John P. Meier notes in his commentary on Matthew, 'It is also the heart of the sermon.'

The version before us today is the shorter one of Luke. Luke and Matthew give us the particular form of the Our Father that each is familiar with. It is the version that, presumably, was the liturgical form of the prayer as used by the congregation each apostle came to be in charge of.

The prayer takes the form of two sets of petitions. The first set refers to God, and the second set to our needs. Jesus teaches us to address God as Father, in Matthew as Our Father. The former may be the original version; the latter may reflect its reformulation in the later church. Either way it is an invitation to approach God not as a distant God or as the majestic Other, but with the intimacy in which Jesus approaches him as the beloved Son.

Jesus teaches us that our first concern must God's concerns and not our own. 'So we are first concerned,' says John P. Meier, 'with the triumph of God's cause.' As loving children, our concern is for our Father's desires, that 'he will fulfil his purposes in the world, as they already are achieved in heaven.' (*Oxford Dictionary of the Bible*) And so we pray that God's name will be hallowed, that God will be blessed and praised on earth as he is blessed and praised already and each moment by the angelic hosts in heaven.

And we pray that his will may be done, obediently and lovingly, on earth as it is done obediently and lovingly by the angels in heaven. In praying thus we are praying for the success of Christ's mission of redemption, and for the flowering of the kingdom of God on earth.

The prayer now moves from our Father's desires to our own needs. We ask for our daily bread. We ask for the daily food that sustains us and our families. We may extend the meaning of bread here to include our general welfare. For if we lack bread and general welfare we cannot sustain our lives and our families, nor can we worship God and pursue his kingdom adequately. But we must ask with confidence. If our loving Father provides for the birds of the air and the lilies of the field, how much more will he not provide for his loving children when they turn to him for their daily sustenance? (cf Lk 12: 22-31)

We ask his forgiveness of our sins. We ask on the basis of our own forgiveness of those who offend us. John P. Meyer notes that mutual forgiveness among the disciples of Jesus is a precondition of God's forgiveness on the last day.

We pray that we not succumb to temptation but are delivered from evil. These are two ways of saying the same thing. Daniel J. Harrington interprets this as a petition 'that in the time of testing accompanying the coming of God's kingdom we may not fall prey to the Evil One.' Meier calls it a petition that in 'the terrible outbreak of moral chaos and violence just before the end, when the powers of evil would seem to gain the upper hand over the disciples, they [and we] pray that God will spare them [and us] the full impact of this final test.'

Perhaps the core of the great 'test' or 'trial' or 'temptation' is the attack on faith and the decline of faith. We recall that Jesus once asked the sobering question, 'When the Son of Man comes [again], will he find faith on earth?' (Lk 18:8) Our withstanding of the attacks on faith, in these the last days, is the deliverance we most pray for in the Lord's Prayer. For all of that, I think we may pray for other deliverances as well. May we be delivered in the temptations that spring from our human weaknesses and from our poverty. May we be given the grace to withstand each day's temptations and the grace to survive the test of whatever substantial cross life may ask us to carry.

The Rich Man Called Fool

[Jesus] said to them, 'Take heed, and beware of all covetousness; for a man's life does not consist in the abundance of his possessions.' And he told them a parable, saying, 'The land of a rich man brought forth plentifully; and he thought to himself, "What shall I do, for I have nowhere to store my crops?" And he said, "I will do this: I will pull down my barns, and build larger ones; and there I will store all my grain and my goods. And I will say to my soul, Soul, you have ample goods laid up for many years; take your ease, eat, drink, be merry." But God said to him, "Fool! This night your soul is required of you ..."'

The late Duchess of Windsor is supposed to have said, 'One can never be too thin or too rich.' She was herself quite thin and very rich. I think most people would agree with her. On the other hand, G. K. Chesterton wrote, 'The rich are the scum of the earth in every country.' (*The Flying Inn*) Tough words indeed!

Perhaps we Christians are ambivalent about riches. Perhaps we're not too clear on where we're supposed to stand in relation to them. We remember, for one thing, hearing the words of Jesus, 'It is easier for a camel to go through the eye of a needle than for a rich man to enter the kingdom of God.' (Mt 19:24) And we remember the story of poor Lazarus, covered in sores licked by the street dogs, who lay by the gate of the rich man's house hoping for a few scraps to fall from his table. We may even wonder (since the gospel does not tell us) whether Lazarus or the street dogs won the battle of the scraps. We do remember, however, that when the poor man died he was carried by the angels to heaven, whereas when the rich man died 'he was buried in hell.' (Lk 16:22) Tough words again about the rich!

Yet Jesus did not scorn the rich. He dined in the homes of the socially well-off Pharisees (Lk 7:36; 11:37) and even in the home of one of their leaders (14:1). Then there was Joseph, a member of the Sanhedrin or high priests' council, 'a wealthy man of Arimathea' (Mt 27:57), who was a secret disciple of Jesus and in whose tomb Jesus was buried.

If the Lord does not condemn riches as such why does he appear to warn so strenuously against them on several occasions?

Perhaps it's because human beings handle riches so poorly. Riches make fools of most of us. They are a challenge and a danger. The challenge is to use riches wisely; the danger is that they tend to consume our souls. As you well know, money is our standard of exchange. We use it for buying and selling. If one has much money one can buy almost anything – and anyone. Look at the super-rich Colombian drug barons of our day! They hold their country and its people in perpetual ransom. Or look at our own recent land rezoning shenanigans! These illustrations tell us that money is not just a standard of exchange but a measure of power. And as Lord Acton once noted, 'Power tends to corrupt.' (*Historical Essays and Studies*)

In today's gospel incident, the rich man called Fool is destroyed by his riches and possessions. He is driven to destruction by his 'covetousness'. He is destroyed by avarice. A heart full of greed is a heart with no room for God or for people in it. It is a heart on the road to spiritual ruin. In his *Aeneid* Virgil looks at the human lust for gold and says of it, 'To what cannot you compel the hearts of men!' In the gospel Jesus looks at covetousness and says in effect, 'To what cannot you compel the souls of men and women!'

In the story of the rich man called Fool covetousness and the love of riches gave him overflowing barns and warehouses for sure, but they left him spiritually empty. He was unprepared when God's call to judgement came: 'Fool! This night your soul is required of you.' Are we, then, to avoid riches like the plague? No. But we are to tell ourselves that riches are a challenge and they can be a danger. And we are to tell ourselves that we must never allow our riches to define us or set bounds of exclusion in the face of God and people. We are to tell ourselves that our Christian faith already defines us and, therefore, that our first concern is for the rule of God over our hearts and the practice of the kingdom virtues of love and justice in our dealings with others. If this be how things stand with us, then any material riches we have or acquire will never remake our Christian image in the image of the gospel's Fool.

The Call to be Holy

[Jesus said], 'Let your loins be girded and your lamps burning, and be like men [and women] who are waiting for their master to come home from the marriage feast, so that they may open to him at once when he comes and knocks.'

We are the servants Jesus speaks of in today's gospel parable. We are wise and faithful servants when we tend to our Christian obligations as we wait for the Lord's coming. We are foolish and unfaithful servants if we don't. We are the servants who are prepared for our Master's return, or the servants who are not. John P. Meier rightly calls this parable a 'parable of vigilance' in his commentary on Matthew.

Jesus tells us to have our loins girded, i.e. our belts tightened, in preparation for his coming. People in the Middle East wore a long loose robe because of the heat. When they worked in the fields they shortened the robe by tucking it up at the waist. They held the tuck in place by tightening their belt. And in their homes they trimmed or replaced the wick of the lamp every so often so as to keep the light burning brightly. These images of the tucked robe and the trimmed wick suggest keen attention to the work of our Christian calling, and the absence of idleness and neglect.

What is our Christian calling? It is holiness. The scripture tells us that God chose the Hebrew people from among all the nations of old for a specific purpose – to be different from all the others by being particularly like himself. God himself is above all else holy. He wanted the Hebrews to be holy as he himself is holy. He told them, 'You shall make and keep yourselves holy, for I, the Lord your God, am holy.' (Lev 11:44) Chapters 17 through 26 of Leviticus make up the so-called Holiness Code. Its teachings derive from the Hebrew people's understanding of the holiness of God and on how best to pattern themselves after him. And rightly so, because holiness is 'characteristic of the divine essence.' (Rahner-Vorgrimmler, *Theological Dictionary*)

Of you and me, the new people of God, Paul says, 'God has saved us and has called us to a holy life.' (2 Tim 1:9) Peter says, 'Become holy yourselves in every aspect of your conduct, after the likeness of the one who called you ... "Be holy, for I am holy".' (1 Pet 1:15-16) Again Peter says, 'You, therefore, are a chosen race, a royal priesthood, a holy nation, a people God claims for his own.' (2 Pet 2:9) The *Catechism of the Catholic Church* states, 'All Christians in any state or walk of life are called ... to holiness: "Be perfect, as your heavenly Father is perfect" (Mt 5:48).' (#2013) You and I, then, by our Christian calling and grace, already participate in the holiness of God, and are called to increase it. It is surely a free and a staggering gift but it is also a task to be worked at and completed.

Most of us blanch at the task. Perhaps we blanch because we see holiness as something only for mystics and canonised saints and the marvellously graced and gifted. Or perhaps we blanch because we know ourselves too well and we have long since settled for 'also ran' in the race for holiness. Or perhaps we confuse holiness with 'heroic' holiness and so are discouraged from even lining-up at the start gate. The Little Flower's holiness consisted in no more than being a child in her Father's presence and in doing the little things and the humdrum things in a spirit of trust, love and worship. Assuming our Father's co-operating grace – and we may assume it confidently – Thérèse's 'little way' is a simple yet beautiful plan of holiness within the capacity of any of us. God knows there's plenty of the humdrum in housework and diaper-changing, or in commuting and computing, day in and day out!

The *Catechism of the Catholic Church* suggests another plan of holiness: the practise of the traditional virtues. And what are they after all but the commandment of love broken down into specific attitudes and actions? The Sermon on the Mount, too, is an entire programme of holiness. Whichever way of holiness we adopt – the 'little way,' or the 'way of the virtues,' or the 'way of the beatitudes' – we will find that holiness is a way of walking with God and of loving the neighbour all our days.

The Divisive Christ

[Jesus said], 'I came to cast fire upon the earth; and would that it
were already kindled! ... Do you think that I have come to give peace
to the earth? No, I tell you, but rather division; for henceforth in
one house ... they will be divided father against son and son against
father, mother against daughter and daughter against mother,
mother-in-law against daughter-in-law and daughter-in-law
against mother-in-law.'

Some of the early writings of the church, after the time of the
apostles, are called 'apologies'. They are not apologies in the
modern sense but defences or explanations of the faith.
Christians had to defend and explain themselves to established
Judaism, and later to their critics and to the authorities of the
Roman empire. Cardinal Newman used the word in this sense
when he wrote his *Apologia Pro Vita Sua*.

The fact that the early Christians had to resort to these apologies underlines the strength of the opposition they faced and the
truth of Jesus' assertion in today's gospel that he had not come
to bring peace 'but rather division'.

Even in the happy event of Our Lord's presentation as a child
in the temple, the prophet Simeon said to Mary, 'This child is set
for the fall and rising of many in Israel, and for a sign that is spoken against, and a sword will pierce your own heart also.' (Lk 2:
34-35) The coming of Jesus would bring sorrow amid joy. He
would divide families and friends and even a whole nation over
the issue of who should receive their primary love and loyalty.
Our Lord is in no doubt about who should receive them. He, the
Lord of life and love, should receive them.

We know from history that Jesus divided families. We can
understand this rather easily. Imagine a Jewish husband converting to Christianity and imagine the religious and cultural
friction that action occasioned for everyone in the family.
Imagine, in later years, the wife of a Roman officer converting to
Christianity and the consequences of that action for her husband
as a man sworn in loyalty to Caesar-God. No doubt it introduced the living of a secret life in some instances, and no doubt
it caused the break-up of some marriages, making way for the

so-called Petrine and Pauline 'privileges' in the annulment
processes of the Catholic church.

Division and the sword are present in our lives as followers
of Jesus, and we should not try to avoid the challenge and the
pain they represent. If, for example, you are committed to the
pro-life agenda, you may find others on the street where you
live who are not. If you are guarded about the latest visionary
and faith-healer, you may be confronted by parishioners who
worry about your lack of faith in the messages of Our Lady. If
you are scrupulous about your taxes, you may find friends and
relations who regard you as extreme. If you refuse to pay for
some services 'in cash under the table,' you may wait a long time
to have your phone call returned when you need these same services again. If you challenge our persistent irresponsibility with
public monies, you may find yourself known in the county
buildings or in the neighbourhood as a bit of a pest – and if you
keep at it, as a bit of a Protestant. This, of course, is not intended
as a tribute to Protestant honesty but as a cultural slight to you.

John P. Meier, in his commentary on Matthew's version of
today's gospel passage, notes that 'to be worthy of Jesus one
must place no one and nothing above him.' Daniel J. Harrington
writes that the passage is 'not an attack on family life as such,
but it does insist that the disciples have a greater loyalty to Jesus
than to the members of their families. In the extreme case of having to choose between Jesus and one's family, Jesus demands
absolute loyalty to himself.' You and I may never be called to
make such an extreme choice. And we may never be asked to
lose our life for Jesus as he lost his life for us, but we are called
every day to challenges and to choices, sometimes quite difficult, in order to safeguard his primacy among the loyalties and
loves of our hearts.

The Narrow Door

And someone said to him, 'Lord, will those who are saved be few?'
Jesus said to them, 'Strive to enter by the narrow door; for many, I
tell you, will seek to enter and will not be able. When once the
householder has risen up and shut the door, you will begin to stand
outside and knock at the door, saying, "Lord, open to us." He will
answer you, "I do not know where you come from." Then you will
begin to say, "We ate and drank in your presence, and you taught
in our streets." But he will say, "I tell you, I do not know where you
come from; depart from me, all you workers of iniquity!" ... And
men will come from the east and west, and from north and south,
and sit at table in the kingdom of God. And behold, some are last
who will be first, and some are first who will be last.'

The biblical commentators tell us that the teaching on the kingdom of God is the central message of the life of Jesus. The kingdom, i.e. the reign of God, his rule of love and peace and justice
in our hearts, is much the same thing as salvation. To bring salvation to the people was to prepare them for, and place them in,
the kingdom of God. Over the generations, however, salvation
has often been restricted to mean just one aspect of it, such as
being saved from hell or promised heaven.

The question, 'Lord, will those who are saved be few?'
means, 'Are they few who enter the kingdom?' A Jew asking this
question had no concept of heaven (or the hereafter) as we understand it. The Jewish inquirer, in his historical and religious
context, was asking about reconciliation with God in the present
time, about insurance against the dread aspects of 'day of the
Lord,' and about membership in the restored and glorious kingdom of David here on this earth.

Our Lord's answer must have startled his Jewish inquirer.
Jesus tells him, 'Strive to enter by the narrow door.' The man
must have asked himself why should he? For he is of the chosen
people. He has Abraham for his father. He is a child of the
promise. He should be able to breeze through into the kingdom
on the strength of his religious pedigree. Yet it is of this man and
his fellow-Jews that Jesus cautions, 'Many will seek to enter and
not be able to do so.' It will do them no good to invoke their an-

cestry, or to protest that they ate and drank in his presence, and that he taught in their streets, i.e. that they and he are well-known to each other. For all of that, they will enter the kingdom only on the terms set down by John the Baptist, the herald of the kingdom. Those terms are repentance, acceptance of the gospel, commitment to the love, peace and justice of the kingdom, and the faith and heart of a child.

Jesus startles his Jewish inquirer further. People will come from the east and the west and the north and the south and find a place in the kingdom. These people are the hated Gentiles. It is their faith in Jesus, and their acceptance of his gospel, that will win them their place. In context, 'the first' and 'the last' are the Jews and the Gentiles, the chosen people and the pagans. The Jews are first in that the gospel is first preached to them. They are 'the natural heirs of the kingdom.' (Mt 8:12) Yet, as Jesus says in today's gospel, 'You will weep and gnash your teeth when you see Abraham and Isaac and Jacob and all the prophets in the kingdom of God, and people from east and west and north and south, and you yourselves excluded.' Gentiles, the last, will take your place instead!

And what of us? Being known as a Christian is not, these days, a guarantee of membership in the kingdom of God; for there may be as many nominal as committed Christians, and nearly every rogue in the land that makes the news in negative fashion is, statistically speaking, a baptised, communioned and confirmed one. Relying on the faith and the sufferings of our Catholic and Protestant forebears guarantees nothing either, for the salvation of each of us is not a matter of our ancestors' faith but of our own personal acceptance of the Lord Jesus, his gospel, and his grace.

Finally, there is the sense of the first and the last from the point of view of worldly attainment and measurement. People who are first in the eyes of this world, and in their own eyes, may be last in terms of the kingdom and in the eyes of God.

The image of the narrow door through which Jesus bids us enter his kingdom is not, I suspect, so much an icon of difficulty as an image of concentrated focus on the few things that count. Those few things are repentance; acceptance of the Lord Jesus, his gospel and his grace; commitment to the love, peace and justice of his kingdom; and the trust and heart of a little child.

Is Humility Humbug?

One sabbath when [Jesus] went to dine at the house of a ruler who belonged to the Pharisees, they were watching him ... He told a parable to those who were invited, when he marked how they chose the places of honour, saying to them ... 'Every one who exalts himself will be humbled, and he who humbles himself will be exalted.'

Since Jesus is invited to dine in the house of a ruler of the Pharisees we may assume that other Pharisees were invited too. These are most likely the ones who were 'watching him'. Why were they watching him? Most likely to see if he would, once again, perform a healing on the sabbath and so break the law.

Similarly, Jesus is 'watching them'. He is observing how they all want the places of honour, the prominent seats, at the dinner table. He determines to teach them a lesson in humility. He does so by telling two parables.

The second of these parables is the parable in the gospel reading for today. It is a parable about the seating arrangements at a wedding feast. You should not presume, Jesus tells the Pharisees, to seat yourself in the place of honour lest that seat be allotted to someone more distinguished than you, and the host is forced to humiliate you in public by directing you to the lowest seat. On the other hand, if you sit in the lowest place your host may invite you up higher and you will thereby gain honour in front of everyone. In other words, be humble. If you are to be exalted, let your exaltation be done for you by others.

Humility is problematical for us. The pull and drag of life does not promote humility nor incline us to favour it. For life is very competitive. It cautions us that the humble usually get trampled on. It endorses the observation of the anonymous General who said that humility never won a war. It agrees with the caustic wit of the oil billionaire, J. Paul Getty, who is supposed to have said, 'The meek shall inherit the earth, but not the mineral rights.' Can you imagine a county football or hurling coach giving the lads a pep talk on humility at half-time and expecting them to win the All-Ireland on the basis of it? How many megastars of song, screen or sport humbly attribute their talent to God? For that matter, how many of us Christians are convinced that all we are and have is pure gift and grace of God? I don't believe that things have changed all that much since the time of Jesus and the puffed-up Pharisees. There's still an awful lot of jockeying for prominence in society and even in the church. There's still a lot of posturing in our living and loving, and in our serving and worshipping. We give notional assent, of course, to humility. As followers of the Lord we have to. But most of us are bent a bit – maybe even 'devastated' or 'gutted,' to use contemporary buzz words – when the praises and the honours and the medals and the gongs are passed out, and we are passed over.

In exalting humility I don't wish to undermine the right of peers or of society to praise a life and a talent spent in the service of others, or the importance of celebrating those worthy of celebration because they mirror the goodness and the gifts of God in their lives for the sake of others. I do not think that Jesus wished to undermine the right either. I believe he was warning us against the presumption of eminence on our part. In doing so, he was not condemning the right of others to recognise us and our worth should they so wish.

In this, Jesus is faithful to the wisdom that his mother and foster-father, as good Jewish parents, would have taught him. A major part of that wisdom is called the Book of Proverbs. In that book we find a parallel to Jesus' teaching on humility in today's gospel: 'Let another praise you – not your own mouth; someone else – not your own lips.' (27:2)

The Cost of Discipleship

Now great multitudes accompanied him; and he turned and said to them, 'If anyone comes to me and does not hate his own father and mother and wife and children and brothers and sisters, yes, and even his own life, he cannot be my disciple. Whoever does not bear his own cross and come after me, cannot be my disciple.'

On becoming the wartime Prime Minister, Winston Churchill said, 'I have nothing to offer but blood, toil, tears and sweat.' (*The Churchill War Papers*, 2) Jesus, in today's gospel, turns to the great multitudes of would-be disciples and offers them the cross.

But Churchill did not offer his people only blood, toil, tears and sweat. He offered them the hope of victory too. And Jesus did not invite prospective disciples to carry their crosses without purpose, but in the hope of glory. If, in Christ, there is no crown without the cross, neither is there the cross without the crown.

What is the cross? It can be as plain as the petty pace of life, as ordinary as the common burdens of each day shouldered with faith. It can be a particular and substantial cross such as living with grave injustice or cancer or AIDS, or living without the spouse one married or without the child lost to suicide. Or it can be the regional cross, so to speak, of surviving in a place where war and famine are cyclical, or it can be the local cross of surviving in a neighbourhood where gangs and violence, thugs and drugs, have put down seemingly indestructible roots.

It can be the cross of what the old spiritual writers called 'my predominant passion'. This cross is the particular weakness or the particular disposition (a quick temper, a sarcastic tongue) that keeps getting me into trouble and depresses my own spirit. It can be the 'monkey on my shoulder,' my addiction to whatever substance is dangerous to me and anti-social. The struggle to be free of such a cross is a heavy cross indeed.

Perhaps a worthwhile cross is found these days in just living a simple or substantially less consumerist lifestyle, in taking a counter-cultural stand with regard to possessions and things, in advocating solidarity with the least and the disadvantaged in society, and in fearlessly upholding the right to life of those who cannot speak for themselves at either end of the spectrum of life?

When Jesus told his would-be disciples that they must hate their nearest and dearest in order to be true disciples of his, he was not, of course, speaking literally. He could not have been. He was not a hawker of hate and a destroyer of family life. He was the prince of love, and love's greatest exponent. He was merely stating that loyalty to him may require the most major of sacrifices from those who follow him. This is the proverbial 'cost of Christian discipleship'.

This cost of Christian discipleship may mean only small sacrifices as we lose a friend here or an acquaintance there in the cut and thrust over Christian principles and ethical behaviour. On the other hand, it may mean major losses, and even the loss of our lives. We remind ourselves that the annals of the saints include a hefty list of martyrs, and there has been no shortage of Christian martyrs around the world in the decades in which we have lived our lives.

When Jesus spoke his words about the disciple carrying his or her cross, he was on his way to Jerusalem to accept his own cross, and to carry it on his shoulders to Calvary. At such a critical time for him, he was looking for real disciples who would shoulder their crosses in imitation of him, and in solidarity with him. He was not looking for camp followers and fair weather friends. He was looking for true disciples and faithful friends. Let us carry our crosses, whatever they be, in union with him. And let us not forget that our cross, as his, is more than a cross. Its reach is beyond itself. It is an instrument of Christian identification, of grace and even of glory.

The Searcher

Now the tax collectors and sinners were all drawing near to hear him. And the Pharisees and the scribes murmured, saying, 'This man receives sinners and eats with them.' So Jesus told them this parable: 'What woman, having ten silver coins, if she loses one coin, does not light a lamp and sweep the house and seek diligently until she finds it? And when she has found it, she calls together her friends and neighbours, saying, "Rejoice with me, for I have found the coin which I had lost." Just so, I tell you, there is joy before the angels of God over one sinner who repents.'

The Pharisees and the scribes are shocked by Jesus. He does something unheard of among orthodox people. He welcomes sinners and eats with them. In the orthodox view, sinners must be avoided at all cost. They are not people to be welcomed or to be saved but people 'deserving of destruction,' as Barclay notes in his commentary.

Jesus tells three parables in explanation of his behaviour. In doing so, he radically re-adjusts the theology of the Pharisees and the scribes and the orthodox. He is teaching them that God does not avoid sinners; that God actually loves sinners; and that God actively searches them out in order to save them.

Sinners are not doomed: they are just lost. God wants them back. And so we have three stories about loss: the story of the lost sheep, the story of the lost coin, and the story of the lost son. In each case, someone grieves over what is lost and that some-one searches in the hope of finding. The good shepherd leaves the ninety-nine sheep and searches for the one lost sheep 'until he finds it'. The grieving father goes to a piece of high ground, presumably every day, to scan the horizon for his lost son. That is why he is able to see his son returning even when the lad is still 'at a distance'. The diligent woman lights a lamp and sweeps the house until she finds her lost coin.

You and I, in this age of the decent pay packet, might wonder about a woman beside herself over the loss of a single coin. We presume it's just a small silver coin in an area of the world where silver was not a scarce commodity. We presume it's just a piece of common coinage. So why the woman's frantic search?

Barclay's suggestion is plausible. He believes the coin is a silver drachma – worth much less than a Euro or a dollar today. The floor of the woman's house would have been an earthen floor covered with reeds. She lights the lamp, he says, so she might catch the glint of the small coin, and she sweeps the floor that she may hear the coin tinkle as it moves.

The coin may have been precious to the woman because it stood between her family and hunger, or it may have been precious for a romantic reason. Barclay notes that the sign of a married woman was a headpiece above her eyes made of ten silver coins linked in a silver chain. These linked coins were so precious, because of what they represented in terms of marriage and family life, that the law forbade their confiscation even as payment of a just debt. It may have been one of these coins that the woman lost, and today's equivalent would be the loss of a wedding ring. No wonder she searches, and no wonder she rejoices when she finds the coin.

God, says Jesus, is like that. God is like the diligent woman when it comes to searching for the precious sinner and rejoicing with the angels when he or she is found. And God is like the good shepherd who leaves the ninety-nine sheep to go out and search the ledges and the ravines for the single one that is lost. And God is like the forgiving father who goes to the piece of high ground and scans the horizon every day for the sight of his prodigal child.

Dear friends, we need to let these stories that Jesus told sink in. We need to delight in the wonder of which they tell. They are stories about love and longing on God's part, and about our worth and preciousness in his eyes. We need to write our names into these stories because our names belong in them. The Lord is my shepherd. I shall never be without his care. And the Lord is my Father, and he loves me unconditionally.

And I am as precious to him as the marriage coin to the woman who lit her lamp and swept her floor, and rejoiced to put it back in its place before her eyes.

Put Money in its Place!

[Jesus said], 'No servant can serve two masters; for either he will hate the one and love the other, or he will be devoted to the one and despise the other. You cannot serve God and mammon.'

Mammon stands for money or, more precisely, for the worship of money. Mammon was the name of a Syrian god. It was the idol that the Hebrews tried to fashion when they built their golden calf and worshipped it during their exodus from Egypt to the promised land. (see Ex 32)

All of us as Christians have, perhaps, some confusion in our hearts regarding money. We're not quite sure how, as followers of Christ, we should regard it. Is it a good thing or a bad thing? We've heard it said that the Bible condemns money as the root of all evil. Actually, the Bible doesn't, but a pop song of my childhood does. What the Bible says about money is quite different from what the pop song says. It says, 'the love of money is the root of all evil.' (1 Tim 6:10)

Paul, in context, is advising Timothy on how to deal with the masters of servants and with the wealthier members of his Christian community. Christian masters are not to lord it over their servants, and wealthy believers must not so love money that it becomes the god in their hearts with which Christ must compete. Paul tells Timothy that the 'craving' for money has caused some believers 'to wander away from the faith and has pierced their hearts with many sorrows.' (1 Tim 6:10)

Money in itself is neutral. It's just a medium of exchange. We need it to conduct business and to pay for goods and services. Money can be good or bad depending on how we acquire it, what we do with it, and what it does for us – or to us. Margaret Thatcher once said realistically that 'No one would remember the Good Samaritan if he'd only had good intentions. He had money as well.' (Interview, 6/1/1986) And Somerset Maugham observed that 'money is like a sixth sense without which you cannot make a complete use of the other five.' (*Of Human Bondage*)

On the other hand, the old English essayist Francis Bacon wrote, 'Money is like muck, not good except it be spread.'

(*Essays*) One might not expect such a slurry image from an essayist of the quality of Bacon except it be his emphatic way of warning us against the corrupting character of wealth when it is pursued and hoarded. It is fair to say, I think, that the recent inquiries and tribunals have revealed the slurry side of Irish life and exposed many muddied hands. Money has clearly been the god of choice for many among us in recent times. What we have been watching in our Irish TV stories is the retelling of Paul's advice to Timothy that the obsession with money, the craving for it, makes believers 'wander away from the faith ... their hearts pierced with many sorrows'.

The gospel does not condemn money. Nor does it despise wealth. It does not damn the rich. But it consistently warns of the ease with which money can turn the head and captivate the heart. Money is a very serious matter. It brings with it risk and challenge, and the ethic of responsible management and of generosity. Mammon – the love of money or the craving of it – is another matter. It has compromised people in state and church and prostituted the better instincts of whole nations in their foreign policies. It is a very old god wandering the deserts of old and still wandering the highways and byways of the modern world in search of new worshippers.

Christ gave us the principle by which we need not fear money or wealth or even the god of Mammon. He told us to trust providence and to prioritise God's kingship over our hearts. If we do this all other things in life, including money, will fall into their proper places. The key to how we should handle money in our Christian lives was given us by Jesus when he said, 'Seek first God's kingship over you, his way of holiness, and all these things will be given you besides.' (Mt 6:33 [NAB])

We Have All We Need

[The rich man in hell] said, 'Then I beg you, father Abraham, send [Lazarus] to my father's house, for I have five brothers, so that he may warn them, lest they also come into this place of torment.' But Abraham said, 'They have Moses and the prophets; let them listen to them.' And he said, 'No, father Abraham; but if someone goes to them from the dead, they will repent.' He said to him, 'If they do not hear Moses and the prophets, neither will they be convinced if someone should rise from the dead.'

On New Year's eve I heard someone on the radio comment on the increasing brawling and drunken disorder in our streets 'after hours'. He said something like this: 'We are starting a new year – indeed a new social era – when our young people have nothing to direct their behaviour. The church's authority has self-destructed and so far nothing has taken its place.'

In today's gospel we have two characters, the rich man traditionally called Dives and the poor man called Lazarus (in Hebrew, Eleazar). The rich man is dressed in fine linen and feasts sumptuously every day. The poor man lies at the rich man's gate every day, full of sores licked by the street dogs, contending with them for the scraps that fall from the rich man's table. There is no personal contact between the rich man and the poor man. There is no indication that the rich man even notices the poor man. And maybe that is the story's first lesson for us: our need to notice the poor and the migrants, and stretch out our hands and our hearts to them.

When Dives and Lazarus die, as inevitably all of us will, the one is buried in hell and the other is brought to heaven. According to our story, there is a fixed chasm between heaven and hell so that no one can cross from one place to the other. Each place is a final stop, and there are no transfers. That is the second lesson: the absence of opportunity once this life is over and, therefore, our need to seize the present time with its saving grace. As St Paul said to his convert Corinthians, 'Behold, now is the acceptable time; now is the day of salvation.' (2 Cor 6:2)

There follows, in the story, a discussion between the rich man and Abraham, the father of the Jewish people. It centres on the critical importance of salvation, and on the means by which to attain it. The doomed rich man has five living brothers and he wants Abraham to send Lazarus to them so they may repent in time and be saved. Abraham refuses. He says, 'They have Moses and the prophets; let them follow them.' If they do, they will be saved. But the rich man thinks this is not enough. If Lazarus is sent to them from 'the other side' that will surely convince and convert them. Again, Abraham refuses. If they will not listen to Moses who brought them God's Law, and to the prophets whom God sent to explain the Law, all the less will they listen to a poor beggar returning from the dead.

There is a lesson here too, the lesson that we have a sufficiency of guides and graces to save us, if we would only use them. Bertrand Russell once said that God hasn't given us enough signs of himself. Perhaps there are millions in the Western world like Russell. They would believe if God only gave more signs of his existence and his love. Perhaps our own faith and love would be all that more vibrant if God spoke directly to us, or if Christ walked our streets today as surely as he did the streets of Nazareth. Perhaps today's gospel story had Russell's 'if only' and all our other 'ifs' in mind, and is an answer to them. At any rate, it tells those of us gifted with the faith that enough is given for the living of a faith-filled and loving life.

'They have Moses and the prophets,' Abraham said to Dives of his brothers, 'let them listen to them.' We of the household of the faith have more than Moses and the prophets to listen to: we have Jesus to guide us and to grace our way. We have the fullness of God's word and grace in him. And so, we are able to agree with John who wrote in his gospel: 'From his fullness we have all received, grace upon grace. For the law was given through Moses; grace and truth came through Jesus Christ. No one has ever seen God; the only Son, who is in the bosom of the Father, he has made him known.' (Jn 1:16-17)

Lord, Increase our Faith!

The apostles said to the Lord, 'Increase our faith!' And the Lord said, 'If you had faith as a grain of mustard seed, you could say to this sycamore tree, "Be rooted up, and be planted in the sea," and it would obey you.'

'We walk by faith, not by sight,' says Paul the Apostle. (2 Cor 5:7) The *Catechism of the Catholic Church* agrees. It stresses the church's role in our faith. 'Believing is an ecclesial act. The church's faith precedes, engenders, supports and nourishes our faith.' (#181) This is fine theology, but there are individuals whose personal faith has not been supported and nourished by the church in, for example, the child abuse saga. If the Catholic Church is to be a believable institution, never mind one which supports and nourishes people's faith, 'it will have to become a – sight more Christian,' said a One-In-Four victim on Prime Time.

If believing is an ecclesial act it is primarily a personal act. It is my response to the gift offered me by God. The church of recent years is being forced to adopt a more modest estimate of its role in our faith. It must itself learn again to be an honest and trusting disciple of Jesus if it is to help others 'walk by faith and not by sight.' (2 Cor 5:7)

Today's short gospel speaks to each one of us about faith, and to the church in general, and to the church at the level of its authority.

The context of today's short gospel is not given by Luke but by Matthew. A man brings his epileptic boy to the disciples because Jesus is not present at the time. The boy's condition is attributed to the presence of a demon. Jesus has already given the disciples power over evil spirits, yet they fail to free the boy of his demon. The father then goes to Jesus, trusting him absolutely. Later, when the disciples are alone with Jesus, they ask him, 'Why were we not able to cast out the demon?' Jesus tells them, 'Because of the littleness of your faith.'

John P. Meier notes (in his Matthew commentary) that little or small faith is the favourite theme of Matthew. 'The little faith of the disciples is a faith which understands but which does not trust God totally. A faith which trusts God can be, in the world's estimation, as small and unimpressive as a mustard seed. Yet such trust can do the impossible, as the hyperbolic image of moving mountains [and planting trees in the sea] stresses.' Barclay says, 'We see here the central need of faith, without which nothing can happen.' Our Lord is not telling us that if our faith is intense and our trust in God deep we will be able to do spectacular things against the order of nature: he is telling us that the pastoral challenges we face, and even the hardest spiritual tasks, can be resolved and accomplished by pure faith even if that faith is only the size of the small mustard seed. It is not quantity that matters in faith, but purity.

Perhaps you and I – and the church of recent days – hedge our bets. We lift up one hand in faith but withhold the other. We have one leg planted in our faith and the other in the ways of the world. We have faith but it's not as steady as it might be. We trust in the Lord but perhaps it's less than the wholehearted trust of a child. How often do we not see this one-handed, one-legged faith in our personal lives and in the face of our pastoral challenges!

We are disciples, i.e. learners, in all things, and for the full length of our lives. We are disciples in the ways of faith. Our own life stories, and the life story of the church, tell us that we are still short of Paul's rule that we walk by faith and not by sight. We are still short of the trusting nature of the child to whom, said Jesus, the kingdom of God belongs. Let us ask for such faith today, knowing that if we ask wholeheartedly we will receive it.

Gratitude

As he entered a village, he was met by ten lepers, who stood at a dis-
tance and lifted up their voices and said, 'Jesus, Master, have mercy
on us.' When he saw them he said to them, 'Go and show yourselves
to the priests.' And as they went they were cleansed. Then one of
them, when he saw that he was healed, turned back, praising God in
a loud voice; and he fell on his face at Jesus' feet, giving thanks.
Now he was a Samaritan. Then said Jesus, 'Were not ten cleansed?
Where are the nine? Was no one found to return and give praise to
God except this foreigner?' And he said to him, 'Rise and go your
way; your faith has made you well.'

There is something about ingratitude that hurts us deeply. We
do good to others, and they respond as if nothing happened. We
spend our lives working for the company, or for the church, and
after a life of service it's as if we were never there. No one says
thanks. Or if they do, it's a perfunctory thing like turning the notice on the shop door from Open to Closed at the end of the day.

Very often it is people who have suffered greatly that are the
truly grateful ones. Elie Wiesel is one of the better-known sur-
vivors of Hitler's Holocaust. He survived the camps, but saw his
whole family die by Nazi hands. In this way he came to discover,
as a mere child, what he calls 'the kingdom of night.' In his
Nobel Prize acceptance speech in Oslo in 1986, he said, 'No one
is as capable of gratitude as one who has emerged from the kingdom of night.'

Now the lepers of Our Lord's time lived in the kingdom of
night. They were so shunned that they had to put distance between themselves and everyone else. They were obliged to wear
a cloth over their mouths and shout 'Unclean! Unclean!' when
anyone approached them. They were not allowed to come near
temple or village synagogue. They were ostracised in life and
even segregated in death. Theirs was the kingdom of night.

Jesus had deep sympathy for these lepers. In today's episode,
ten of them approach him, desperate for a cleansing. He makes
them whole and sends them off to the temple so the priests may
verify their cleansed condition. This was a legal requirement.
Only one of the ten, the Samaritan, the least likely one, comes

back to Jesus to express his gratitude. Our Lord shows his disappointment. 'Were not ten cleansed?' he asks. 'Where are the nine? Was no one found to return and give praise to God except this foreigner?'

Our Lord's disappointment is a challenge to us. Are we grateful? We ought to be. Why? Because we are saved by the grace of God. We are cleansed through baptism. We live securely by Christ's light and love in his kingdom. We are promised an eternal home. So many of our neighbours, in the new social order, must struggle without this faith for today and this hope for tomorrow. These gifts have been given us *gratis* by the loving kindness of our God.

Are we grateful? We ought to be – for the parents who nurtured us and the teachers who educated us; for the doctors who help us and the carers who mind us; for this parish community which helps sustain our faith and hope, and which gathers around us in celebration and support on our days of joy and days of loss.

And are we grateful enough so that we do not assist, in any way, those who create modern-day lepers? We see, in our TV news stories, the racial and religious bigots who treat as lepers those who are not precisely like themselves. Our own mind may be tempted to draw up its list of lepers from among the undisciplined young, the faltering aged, the travellers, the urban poor, the migrants and asylum seekers. Our own heart may be tempted to draw up its list of lepers from among family members, in-laws, old bosses, lost lovers and failed friends.

But let us resist that temptation. There are too many lepers in too many places these days when there should be none at all. The human family is paying a terrible price for persisting with its creation of so many racial, religious and even local neighbourhood lepers. And each one of us is paying a psychological and a spiritual price for his and her list of lepers. You and I harm mostly ourselves when there is a leper, or a list of them, on our mind or in our heart.

Keeping Faith

Jesus told them a parable, to the effect that they ought always to pray and not lose heart ... And he said, 'When the Son of Man comes, will he find faith on earth?'

The persistent widow in today's gospel, who won't take no for an answer, is a 'symbol of all who were poor and defenceless,' says William Barclay. The poor and the defenceless were many in Our Lord's time.

You and I have met these poor and defenceless people again and again in the gospels, Sunday by Sunday. They are the people on the bottom rung of the social ladder. They are the sick, the lame, the blind, the shepherds, the lepers, the religious outcasts, the widow who lost her only son, and the widow who gave away her last penny. They are the ones for whom Jesus has special concern, and in whose regard he shows what the theologians call a 'preferential option.'

The persistent widow in today's gospel is, to me, not only a symbol of all who were poor and defenceless but a symbol of all Christians who persist in prayer and who never weary in their faith in the Lord. For he has named these persistent Christians the poor in spirit, the little ones of God, on account of their faith.

Are we persistent Christians? Are we the little ones of God? These are hard times for us as people of faith in view of the sad stories in our church and in our society. We sense that the church is in crisis. We can react by leaving this church and finding another one, or we can stand our ground and believe that the time of crisis may also be a time of opportunity.

The opportunity that presents itself is the opportunity to practise our faith, not as per usual but in depth. John F. Kennedy said one time, 'When written in Chinese the word crisis is composed of two characters. One represents danger and the other represents opportunity.' (Speech at Indianapolis, 4/12/1959) We should not be believers whose faith is strong or weak on the basis of 'a few bad apples,' a few rogue clerics, or a few bishops not doing their job. What the Bard said of ambition may be said equally of our personal faith: it 'should be made of sterner stuff'. (*Julius Caesar*, 111)

One time the apostles said to Jesus, 'Lord, increase our faith.' (Lk 17:5) That should be our prayer for these times, asking our God to not only preserve our faith but to increase it. In today's gospel Jesus tells the story of the persistent widow so that we 'should pray always and not lose heart'. In another instance, after cleansing the temple and calling it a house of prayer, Jesus told the disciples, 'Have faith in God ... I tell you, whatever you ask in prayer, believe that you have received it, and it will be yours.' (Mk 11:22-24)

Pope John Paul II said in his *Letter to Priests* (27/1/1979): 'Prayer is indeed the source of strength for sustaining what is wavering. It is [in prayer] that there is born a confidence like the confidence expressed by St Paul in the words, "There is nothing that I cannot master with the help of the One who gives me strength" (Phil 4:13).' What the Pope said to priests is well said to all of us. It is in prayer that our faith grows strong and confident.

The last line of today's gospel has a jarring question. Jesus asks, 'When the Son of Man comes, will he find faith on the earth?' Another translation reads, 'Will he find any faith on the earth?' The line has an ominous ring to it, as though the answer might be 'no' or 'very little'. But perhaps the Lord has already answered the question himself in a positive way; perhaps he answered it in telling the story of the persistent widow who never wearied in her request.

The Son of Man will find faith when he comes again, and even deep faith, if each succeeding Christian generation, which is potentially the final generation, prays always and never loses heart.

On Self-Righteousness

[Jesus] told this parable to some who trusted in themselves that they were righteous and despised others: 'Two men went up to the temple to pray, one a Pharisee and the other a tax collector. The Pharisee stood and prayed thus with himself, "God, I thank thee that I am not like other men ..." But the tax collector, standing far off, would not even lift up his eyes to heaven, but beat his breast saying, "God, be merciful to me a sinner!" ...'

Today's gospel lesson is not so much about prayer as about salvation. We do not save ourselves. We do not enter the kingdom, or attain heaven's glory, by telling ourselves how good we are. God alone is the one who makes us righteous. He alone makes us worthy in his eyes.

If we are self-righteous we are, in effect, stating that we are the source of our own salvation. That is why Jesus says that when the Pharisee prayed proudly 'he prayed to himself'. He rattled off the list of his good works like a man delighted to hear the good things he had to say about himself. Our Lord infers that God was not even listening.

The holy city of Kandahar was much in the news when the Taliban were being ousted in Afghanistan. Kandahar was once a part of an ancient Indian empire. An Indian emperor said something there, several generations before the time of Christ, which is similar to what Our Lord says in the gospel today. 'Those who praise themselves and criticise their neighbours are merely self-seekers, who wish to excel but only harm themselves.' (Emperor Asoka, *Proclamation at Kandahar*)

In contrast to the proud Pharisee, the despised tax collector is so aware of his unworthiness that he does not approach the Holy of Holies in the temple but 'stands far off', for he is full of the sense of his sinfulness. He beats his breast and says, 'God, be merciful to me a sinner!'

Today's gospel is about how we see ourselves and how God sees us. To see ourselves as we really are requires humility. But humility is not exactly 'in' at the moment. The language of our time is the language of the self; the language of self-realisation, self-fulfilment, self-assertion and self-promotion. A balanced assertion of the self is, of course, necessary for both healthy living and healthy religious practice. But unbalanced assertions of the self are all too commonplace and are destructive of the self and of the relationships on which the self depends. 'We are all living in the dungeon of self,' observes Cyril Connolly in *The Unquiet Grave*.

Humility is not a weakness: it is an admirable human quality. It keeps us balanced, our feet in reality. It keeps us honest, seeing things as they are and seeing ourselves as we are. Humility tells me where I am strong and weak in my responsibilities as a believer, spouse, parent, pastor, politician, investment broker, teacher, farmer, or student. It tells me there is always room for improvement. It tells me that the gifts and graces I have do not come out of my own pocket. It tells me that I am nothing apart from the others in my life. These others are God and people. I rely on them far more than on myself for whatever it is I am achieving. And I am not justified by myself but by God, and I do not live my life or vocation except through the help and the presence of others. They make what is best in me possible. John Donne keenly observed, 'No man is an Island, entire of itself; every man is a piece of the Continent, a part of the main.' (*Devotions*, 17)

In contrasting the proud Pharisee with the humble sinner, Jesus says, 'Everyone who exalts himself will be humbled.' The humbling will take the form of humiliation sooner or later in this life, or it will be the humility of the day of judgement when we will be read as an open book. Pride was the original sin of the angels and of Adam, and heaven cannot abide it. On the other hand, Jesus says, 'Everyone who humbles himself will be exalted.' We should not be surprised at this. It was because the Son of God emptied himself and 'took the form of a servant' to save us that God 'highly exalted him' in glory. (Phil 2: 5-11) Let us keep in mind the humility and the exaltation of the Son of God so we may see the connection between them, not only in Christ's life but in our own.

Gone Missing

When Jesus came to the place, he looked up and said to him, 'Zacchaeus, make haste and come down; for I must stay at your house today.' So he made haste and came down, and received him joyfully. And when they saw it they all murmured, 'He has gone in to be the guest of a man who is a sinner.' And Zacchaeus stood and said to the Lord, 'Behold, Lord, the half of my goods I give to the poor; and if I have defrauded anyone of anything , I restore it four-fold.' And Jesus said to him, 'Today salvation has come to this house, since he also is a Son of Abraham. For the Son of Man came to seek and to save the lost.'

'Gone missing' is a phrase used on this side of the Atlantic. It is our way of saying that someone is unexpectedly absent. The missing one is not where he or she should be. We hope this to be a temporary condition. These days it is likely to be a young person who's gone missing and, given the dangers of the present time, we are more than a little concerned. We say a prayer, and hope that the missing child shows up very soon.

Today's gospel mentions 'the lost'. Jesus says, 'The Son of Man came to seek and to save the lost.' In the Bible, the lost sometimes means the damned but, with Jesus, it usually refers to sinners who have gone astray. Jesus seeks out these lost ones so they may be found. They are, hopefully, 'gone missing' only temporarily from grace. They are not in the kingdom of God where they ought to be.

In another place, Jesus mentions 'the lost sheep of the house of Israel'. (Mt 15: 24) These, too, are lost temporarily, 'gone missing' from true religion. They have been led astray by the rules and burdens of their leaders, and by the loss of the spirit of the Law. But they remain the children of Abraham and of the promise. As such, they should be seeking Jesus as eagerly as he seeks them. They should be flocking to the kingdom of God. But they are not, except for Zacchaeus.

How do you and I read ourselves into this incident? We are neither the children of Abraham nor children of the Pharisees. In the ninth chapter of the Letter to the Romans, Paul says that the promise of salvation is made not only to the descendants of

Abraham – 'my kinsmen by race' (9:3) – but to whomever God chooses, whether of Jew or Gentile. And he quotes the prophet Hosea (2:23) in that regard, 'Those who were not my people I will call "my people"; and her who was not beloved I will call "my beloved".' For Paul, the promise of salvation falls to anyone, Jew or Gentile, on one condition only. And that condition is faith in Jesus.

The IMF poll of December 2002 states that only 48% of us now attend Mass regularly. The figure has dropped 12% in five years. Regular Mass attendance may not be the best measure of faith in Jesus or of commitment to his gospel, but it is a standard barometer by which Irish faith and practice are measured. In that case, we have a faith problem here in our land. The faith problem is compounded by the fact that no social critic or commentator suggests that this lost faith is being replaced by another form of orthodox religious faith. Faith is receding in the Irish consciousness and, perhaps, Jesus is receding with it.

I hope no future polls add you and me to this list of the lost. I hope that, in response to our gospel of today, we pray from our hearts for perseverance in our faith. I hope that we pray for an ever more vibrant trust in the Lord who saves us day by day. May we pray, too, that those of 'our own' who fill the shadow side of these polls are not among the permanently lost, that they have only gone missing for awhile, and that they are the lost who will be found again.

Resurrection People

And Jesus said to them, 'The sons of this age marry and are given in marriage; but those who are accounted worthy to attain to that age and to the resurrection from the dead neither marry nor are given in marriage, for they cannot die anymore, because they are equal to angels and are sons of God, being sons of the resurrection ... God is not God of the dead, but of the living.'

It's quite a while now since the church began to involve couples in the planning of their wedding ceremony. I remember the first bride-to-be who was so enthusiastic over this new arrangement that she wanted to re-write the entire marriage ritual, especially the vows. She did not wish to marry her intended 'until death do us part' but 'forever'. She was head over heels in love of course. Her intended, I felt, was happy enough with the traditional wording, but he kept very quiet in her presence.

Many years before that, and as a new priest, I kept very quiet myself when an elderly parishioner lost her husband and just could not get over it. She said to me through her tears, 'I do not want to go to heaven unless Harry is there.' And she meant it. As far as she was concerned, heaven could not be heaven without Harry in it. She was dead herself within the year. The loss of Harry was too great a grief for her.

Both of the women just mentioned saw marriage as a bond not only for this life but for the next one as well. The church sees it 'for life' only. (*Catechism of the Catholic Church*, # 1648). Hence the traditional phrase, 'until death do us part'. Jesus says that in the resurrection we neither marry nor are married but are transformed so that we live 'as the angels'. As John P. Meier puts it in his Matthew commentary, 'the physical and sexual relationships of this world [are] transcended' in the next life.

Our Lord's main teaching, however, in today's gospel, is not about marriage but about the fact that there is an afterlife; there is a heaven. What he says about marriage is said in this context, and said only to illustrate his teaching on the reality of the resurrection.

The Sadducees had asked him a question about a woman who had married seven husbands in a succession caused by death. If there is an afterlife, whose wife will she be? After all, seven men married her. The question was supposed to show the silliness of the Pharisees' belief in the resurrection of the body. But in this instance, Jesus sides with the Pharisees. There is a resurrection, he says. There is an afterlife. For God is a living God, and he is God of the living. God lives on and we, consequently, live on too. Death is full stop only to physical life as we know it. There is life after physical death. It is a very changed form of life. You and I call it resurrected life, or the eternal life of heaven.

The Sadducees did not believe in the resurrection because, they claimed, their scriptures did not support it. Besides they were rich and worldly men, and they were wedded to this life, and would be lost without it. They have their counterparts in our present society and in every society.

We know little of the specifics of the afterlife. The scripture paints it with broad strokes, and speaks of it by analogy. Our small knowledge of heaven is due to our inability to visualise heaven as it actually is. We are told that it will be the state of perfect fulfilment and of perfect bliss. We are told it will be an endless rapture in God. We will lack nothing of peace and joy and love. Therefore, we may trust that in some now veiled way we will know again those that we 'have loved long since and lost awhile.' (J. H. Newman, *The Pillar of the Cloud*)

Heaven is the 'place' of our dear Lord's glory, where the Lamb is our shepherd and the Father wipes every tear away. (cf Rev 7:17) Heaven is the 'place' of the promise Jesus made to us, and that promised 'place' – undetailed though it be presently – is enough for me. He said, 'Let not your hearts be troubled; have faith in God and faith in me. In my Father's house are many rooms; if it were not so, would I have told you that I go to prepare a place for you? And when I go and prepare a place for you, I will come again and will take you to myself, that where I am you may be also.' (Jn 14: 1-3)

A Time for Testimony

[Jesus said], 'Take heed that you are not led astray; for many will come in my name, saying, "I am he!" and, "The time is at hand!" Do not go after them ... They will lay their hands on you and persecute you, delivering you up to the synagogues and prisons ... for my name's sake. This will be a time for you to bear testimony.'

One of the central images in the Old Testament is the image of 'the day of the Lord'. You and I meet this image every year in Advent, at the start of the church's liturgical year, and again now at the end of the liturgical year.

The 'day of the Lord' was a central belief of the Jewish generations. Different prophets put their own particular spin on it depending on the time and circumstances in which they lived. Amos, for example, was a prophet of social justice and he, understandably, believed that 'the day of the Lord' would be a day of judgement, judgement in the sense of justice for God's people, and judgement in the sense of condemnation of their oppressors.

I think that 'the day of the Lord,' generally speaking, incorporated the hopes of the small, faithful and oppressed people called the Hebrews. They were always looking to the future in hope. They were always reading the future in terms of freedom and justice and peace and plenty because they were always under one form of bondage or another. Perhaps it's not too far-fetched to compare Jewish history with Irish history and to see the parallel of persistent hope between the Hebrews' 'day of the Lord' and the 'our day will come' (*tiocfaidh ár lá*) of the Irish generations.

The 'day of the Lord' acquired other dimensions besides freedom and justice and hope of the future. The prophet Isaiah envisioned it as a day of terror for sinners. (13:9) The prophet Zephaniah saw it as a day of wrath and ruin afflicting not only the oppressors of Israel but Israel itself. (1: 14-18)

In the early Christian church, 'the day of the Lord' becomes 'the day of the Lord Jesus,' the day of his second coming. In Paul's Letter to the Romans it is a 'day of judgement' also. (2: 12ff) But we may stress the hopeful side of what Paul says about judgement because he does not see judgement as something to be feared by true believers. Paul says that we who are saved by God's grace, through faith in Christ Jesus, are already reconciled to God; therefore we may look forward with confidence to the final judgement. (5: 1-11) And we may look forward with confidence despite the fact that we are tested sorely in this time before the second coming.

Jesus is talking, in today's gospel, about this same time before the second coming. I think you and I realise that we are in it. Ours is the time of testing and of challenge. Our important secular and religious institutions – the so-called institutions of our governance and grace – are themselves subject to audits and inquiries and these things are a challenge to our faith and a testing of it.

We watch members of our families and old friends, perhaps, drop away from faith. Many believers no longer know with any clarity or conviction what the faith entails or what's right and wrong. Would-be prophets and visionaries pop up everywhere, and many believers hang on their every word but will not study the word of God with anything like the same fervour. People rubbish the church and its leadership while others rush to defend them, as if these were the priorities of faith rather than faith's instruments. Jesus is the sole priority of our faith, and 'this,' he said, 'will be a time for you to bear testimony to me.'

Our faith in the Lord Jesus is tested every day, and every day is an opportunity to give testimony to our faith in him. He asks us to testify to his word, not to the word of the latest seer and message bearer. He asks us to give testimony to his life and lifestyle by the likeness of our own to his through grace. He asks us to give testimony to his cross, and not deny it when it enters our lives. He asks us to give testimony to the wideness of his love, not build barriers of exclusion against the least of his sisters and brothers. He asks us to testify to his forgiveness of us through our forgiveness of others.

In the gospel reading four Sundays ago, Jesus asked, 'When the Son of Man comes will he find faith on earth?' (Lk 18:8) Back then I said that we tend to view his question ominously, as though he expects to find little faith or none at all when he comes again. But we can also view it positively should he come, in our time, and find us busy bearing testimony to him.

King and Kingdom

He [the 'good' thief] said, 'Jesus, remember me when you come into your kingdom.' And he said to him, 'Truly, I say to you, today you will be with me in Paradise.'

Paradise is a Persian word. In Persian, it meant a walled or a fruited garden. The Greek Septuagint version of the Bible uses the word to describe the garden of Eden. The garden of Eden was a place of trees and flowers and fruits, and also of innocence and bliss. Our traditional theology of heaven includes the dimension of bliss.

The good thief asks Jesus to remember him when Jesus enters his kingdom. We may assume that the good thief had heard of Jesus' kingdom but understood it in the Persian sense of paradise. People in the Middle East, then as now, knew what paradise meant. Perhaps this is why Our Lord, in his reply, goes along with the good thief's thinking and does not promise him a place in the kingdom but a place in paradise.

All of us attend funerals regularly. We find that the church continues to use the word paradise as a synonym for heaven. At the conclusion of the funeral liturgy in church we hear the priest commend the departed one to God's mercy with the prayer, *In Paradisum* – 'May the angels lead you into paradise.'

Paradise or heaven is, of course, the final aim of our striving and of our faith. Paul, in the first chapter of his Letter to the Colossians, speaks of our hope of heaven. He calls it our 'hope of glory.' (v 27) It is, he says, something assured to those who believe in the Lord Jesus. Even at this moment we hold its promise within ourselves. Therefore, it is critical that you and I remain 'unshaken in this hope that the gospel promises.' (v 23) We must not weaken but maintain our faith in Jesus and continue to practice Christian love. (v 4)

Paul speaks against the background of the attacks on the faith of the Colossians by false teachers and legalistic tendencies. He tells the Colossians that the fullness of redemption and of grace is found in Jesus and, therefore, no spirit or angel (messenger) can add to, or subtract from, this fullness. No novelty, new message, new message bearer or unusual ascetical lifestyle is required beyond the overcoming of our personal sins through grace and loving our neighbour as Christ loved us.

Each Christian generation sees parallels between the situation of the Colossians and itself. Each Christian generation feels threatened by attacks on its faith from the outside and the threat of legalism and various 'enthusiasms' from within. Someone or some group always wishes to change things beyond or beneath the Lord's standards. This Christian generation is no different.

You know the challenges we face. In addition to the normal challenges which religion faces in every generation, there is a certain silence about God in the new Western order which does not help us in our roles as parents and educators. In our society as it is presently shaped, there is poor role modelling in social ethics and personal morals. We feel let down by institutions and personalities we thought were dependable. There is the sense abroad that 'the twilight of the gods' is upon us. But wait! Not all is negative! Good causes and their supporters abound as never before in history, and many nations are doing something not done in the past: they write charity and development aid into their annual budgets. And there are individuals of all ages searching for honest faith, and going to the word of God to find it. And there are still millions, like you, who have a living, vibrant, and loving faith and are more committed nowadays than ever before to directing even the details of their lives by the Spirit and word of the Lord.

On this last Sunday of the liturgical year, the church hails Christ as the universal king. Not all nations and cultures and peoples so acknowledge him, but it is the hope of the gospel that some day they will. For our part, we re-commit ourselves to our Lord and King, and to the advancement of his kingdom on earth. We pray that he may reign more and more by faith and love in our hearts and in our actions so that we may turn our face to his on that as yet hidden day, and hear him say to us, 'Today you will be with me in paradise.'

Mary's Magnificat

Mary said, 'My soul magnifies the Lord, and my spirit rejoices in God my Saviour, for he has regarded the low estate of his hand-maiden. Behold, henceforth all generations will call me blessed; for he who is mighty has done great things for me, and holy is his name. His mercy is on those who fear him from generation to generation.'

I suppose the many Catholic generations have made Mary fit every human need and circumstance. Our hymns and devotions and novenas to Mary cover the range of human need from safe pregnancy to assistance at the hour of death.

In between come such human concerns as finding a letter in the post with sufficient examination points for the university of our choice, finding a job, finding a marriage partner, finding sobriety, finding peace in the home, finding a stray son or daughter who left in a huff, even finding a stray animal in winter. Critics say we overdo 'the Mary thing' and, in the process, steal from her Son who is the sole Saviour. On the other hand, we insist that she is the sole Saviour's mother, and ours too, and so is singularly influential with him in our regard.

Gerard Manley Hopkins understood this. He knew how necessary Mary is to our need. She is as necessary as the air we breathe. And like the air, she is everywhere. She has only one work to do, he said beautifully, and that is to 'Let all God's glory through.' If this is her one work, is it any wonder that we turn to her for everything, and all the time? 'She, wild web, wondrous robe,/ Mantles the guilty globe,/ Since God has let dispense/ Her prayers his providence.' (*The Blessed Virgin Compared To The Air We Breathe*)

While some of our Marian hymns may sound, as someone has said, overly pious and sweet to the male half of Christianity, Mary's own hymn, the Magnificat, is not soft and sweet at all, but powerful. Barclay, in his commentary on Luke, calls it 'the most revolutionary [hymn] in the world', and that is saying quite a lot when we think of such strident hymns as *La Marseillaise* and the *Internationale*. If we wish to honour Mary, let us try to make her hymn our own.

The Magnificat heralds three revolutions, says Barclay. First, it heralds a moral revolution. In the new age that comes with Mary's motherhood of Jesus, pride will be expelled from the hearts of all who follow Christ. Pride is the root sin and the root cause of our moral and social problems. Through Mary's child, pride is overcome and Christian enlightenment and grace take its place.

Second, the Magnificat heralds a social revolution. The mighty, the lords of the earth ones, will be cast down and the poor raised up because of Mary's child. Social position, prestige and honours count for nothing in the new order of Christ. The poor, the lowly and the outcast are lifted up to the measure of their worth and dignity in the eyes of God. We see the work of this social revolution not only in the church but in the better social planning and programmes of many nations.

Third, the Magnificat heralds an economic revolution. Mary's child inspires us as individuals to be less acquisitive and more charitable, and inspires the Western nations, including our own, to give to the less advantaged peoples a percentage of their income. This is a major change in budgeting outlays when we compare this present with the past, and see this infiltration of Christ's heart into the consciousness of so many countries.

'There is a loveliness in the Magnificat,' writes Barclay, 'but in that loveliness there is dynamite. Christianity begets a revolution in each person and revolution in the world.' Perhaps some of us are still tied to a sweet and pious image of Mary because of those sweet and pious hymns we still sing. Perhaps we don't appreciate Mary's depth as a theologian, her strength of character, and the independence of her spirit. All are striking, given the time and place in which she lived and the social position of women then. At any rate, all of us do appreciate her motherhood of God's only Son. And we do appreciate that, as a consequence, he allows her prayers to dispense his providence in our and in our world's regard.

Witnesses

Seeing the crowds, Jesus went up on the mountain, and when he sat down his disciples came to him. And he opened his mouth and taught them, saying, 'Blessed are the poor in spirit, for theirs is the kingdom of heaven ...'

Who are saints? Paul addresses his Letter to the Colossians with these words, 'To the saints at Colossae, faithful brothers [and sisters] in Christ.' (1:2) Paul regarded the members of the church at Colossae – the ordinary parishioners, if you will – as saints, and the standard by which he judged their sanctity was their faithfulness to Christ. By faithfulness to Christ he meant witnessing to Christ.

It is likely that Paul took his definition of witness-as-saint from Christ's own teaching as well as from common Christian usage. John, in his Revelation, describes Jesus as the 'faithful witness'. Luke, in his Acts of the Apostles, recounts Jesus telling the disciples, 'You shall be my witnesses' (1:8), and Matthias is chosen in place of Judas to be 'a witness.' (1:22) Under Paul's norm of witnessing, we in this parish church qualify as saints every bit as much as his own Colossians did.

So, what has happened since the time of Paul and the Colossians that makes saints so special a category in our church, and ourselves so different from them? Why, contrary to Paul and the church of the apostles, does our present church name so few of its members saints? (Many Christian churches, of course, do not make this distinction.)

We may answer by saying that, after the age of the apostles, the church began to restrict the term saint to those who witnessed to their faith by martyrdom. In Revelation 20:4, for example, the martyrs appear as a special group. The church also began to consider as saints only those who were virtuous to an heroic degree. In this way, the apostles' sense of all Christians as 'the saints' or 'the witnesses' was lost. By the fourth century, relatively few Christians were being venerated as saints.

By the tenth century the scene had changed again, not in the sense that all Christians were again recognised as 'the saints', but in the sense that multitudes of supposed miracle workers all

over Europe were. The basis for their status as saints was their
uncritical acceptance by the people. Alleged miracles and heal-
ings (and charlatanry, no doubt) took the place of examined and
proven witness to Christ. In reaction, the church of the tenth to
twelfth centuries introduced the first forms of what would eventually become the process of canonisation.

Under the canonisation process relatively few Christians are
elevated to sainthood and venerated as saints, or ever will be.
For this reason we should regard the canonised saints as – offi-
cially – our most outstanding and heroic models of Christian
witness, but we should not forget Paul's and the scripture's
view that all who witness faithfully to Christ are saints as well.

Some years ago, a friend of mine published a small book entitled, *Saints I Have Known*. The book does not include any canonised saint – or any of the many saints made suspect by legend
and fantasy. The book is about living people whom the author
knows, and I am pleased to say that I know some of them myself. They are ordinary Catholics, ordinary Christians. They live
their lives and their vocations dutifully. They endure their trials,
and sometimes their terrible pain and family tragedies, with
great faith and without any lessening of their love and service of
others. They are constant in worship and in virtue. All that they
do is done to shoulder their share of the cross of Christ and to affirm the hope of resurrection and glory. The power of grace is
manifest in their lives.

The saints, dear friends, are marvellous and they are many.
They are far, far more than the canonised list of our church. If
the total of them were confined to that list, we should have to
conclude that the grace of Christ is far less than it actually is, and
that it has accomplished relatively little over the course of two
Christian millennia. But such, thank God, is not the case. The
saints are marvellous and they are many because Christ's grace
is marvellous and it is much. His saints are as numerous as the
grains of sand on the shore of the bay outside this church building. The saints are the told and the untold, the mass of Christ's
faithful witnesses in every generation. And they are in this generation, and in this parish community, and in this congregation.
And we praise God for all of them, and all of you.

With Confidence

In the sixth month the angel Gabriel was sent from God to a city of Galilee named Nazareth, to a virgin betrothed to a man whose name was Joseph, of the house of David; and the virgin's name was Mary. And he came to her and said, 'Hail, O favoured one, the Lord is with you!'

The immaculate conception means that Mary was preserved free from all stain of original sin from the moment of her conception in her mother's womb. This 'singular grace and privilege,' as Pius IX called it (in *Ineffabilis Deus*), was given to Mary in view of her vocation to be the mother of the world's Saviour. It is unfitting that she who would bring forth the sinless One should herself be stained by sin.

The immaculate conception of Mary in her mother's womb and the virginal conception of Jesus in Mary's womb are necessary parts of the most critical event of our lives – salvation. It is only when we see Mary's privileges in relation to our own needs in salvation and grace that they stop being remote doctrines and big words and become very precious to us.

Mary was given many graces, and most of them have something to do with us. That is why the Holy Father, as the bishop of the diocese of Rome, urged his Roman seminarians to approach Mary with confidence. He called her Our Lady of Confidence when visited them on 12 February 1983. He recounted for them the story of the wedding feast at Cana when the newly-weds ran out of wine.

'What,' he asked, 'were the newly-weds feeling in their hearts at the moment that the wine ran out, as they approached the mother of Jesus?' He answered, 'Confidence, precisely. They had a spontaneous confidence, a confidence that said, "She can help us ... She can help us because she is the Mother, and being a mother she can understand us, she can understand our difficulties and this is the first step to helping ... And, after having understood our difficulties, she will help us".'

When we appreciate that Mary and her motherhood (and her privileges and graces) are integral to God's plan for our salvation, her motherhood reaches beyond the mothering of her Son to the spiritual mothering of all of us.

So let us approach Mary with our hopes and needs and difficulties. Let us approach her as the newly-weds at Cana did, with confidence. Let us remember the water Jesus turned into wine at her request, and the steward's observation that it was the very best of wine. Let us remember the abundance of the wine that was signalled by the six great stone jars, and their symbolism as abundant grace. Let us approach Mary the Mother confidently both now and at the hour of our death. Amen.